Begin.

Open.

Anywhere.

A Journey Through Words

That Will Inspire, Entertain

And Empower You

From Mark Twain to Mother Teresa, Shakespeare to
Cervantes, J.D. Salinger to John Wooden and so many
others, we learn about life.

This book is dedicated to my wife, Diane, the love of my
life, who has always deserved more than I
have been able to give her.

Table of Contents

It may not take a genius to realize that our decisions influence our lives; as Robert Louis Stephenson said, "sooner or later we must all sit down to a banquet of our own consequences."

The genius lies in the ability to communicate the thought with words that brighten our own thoughts on the same subject, words that help us think for ourselves. New ideas and thoughts are typically repackaged old ideas and thoughts. But when they come back to us in our own packaging they render us new; they change us. And we can feel it.

When we decide to "accept", a part of us dies, and a part is born.

We need to focus on the newborn.

One blossom alone may suffice to entice.

Bouquets may prove too few.

The difference is never in number;

the difference is in you.

Character   46

Listen to the eulogies of the wealthy or the brilliant, the athlete or the skilled, and we may feel unconnected, as if they had talents we simply could not develop.

But hear of the man of character, of the good and difficult choices he made throughout his life, and we realize that it comes to all of us not at birth, but one choice at a time, and that no one has an easier path than another on his way to deserving the good eulogy.

Choices   61

No clearer or more well traveled paths exist than the paths leading from our successes or failures back to our choices.

Compassion   72

Every teardrop has a story it shares only with the one who sheds it.

Courage   77

When you start to sweat, when your body shakes, when your heart pounds, when every part of you wishes you were somewhere else, look out—Courage has a chance to be born.

Faith   81

Don't be the unhappy sceptic who looks only
for walking-on-water miracles, and sees none. . . .

Forgiveness 94

Too much emphasis is given to what precedes an act of forgiveness; its magic is in what follows it.

Friendship 104

Friendships more rarely break than whither from neglect.

Attend to a friend.

Gratitude 114

Sometimes all we need to do
is envision her wrapped in a ribbon—
to remind ourselves
of just how precious she is.

Happiness 137

Happiness: Always to be found where you need to be looking—outward.

Humor 141

If you're going through a difficult time in your life and someone says, "you'll laugh about this in 30 years," it's not the 30 years that will work the magic; it's the laughter.

Imagination   157

At some point I stopped being Superman and Davy Crockett, but each of them taught me how to think, how to dream, how to imagine greatness in my life, and I am thankful to both of them for helping my imagination stay close enough to my talents to make at least a little sense, yet far enough away from them to stretch those talents. That's what imagination is for.

Language   164

Hearing the right language at the right time is like looking into the right eyes at the right time … in the right room.

Life   169

It's a carnival where you don't get to pick the rides, except for the roller coaster. And anytime you want, you can step up and take a chance for that teddy bear. Usually, the teddy bear is safe.

Love   203

Those who chooses to love the parts when he can't love the whole improves not only the whole, but his life as well.

Parental Encouragement 217

Parents' words echo in the minds of their children long after the parents have gone. And they don't only echo, in the sense that the words are repeated. They come back to us in an exalted, weightier form, often with lessons and language our parents never dreamed of.

Parenting 227

A good parent is someone whose children may be average, but, if they are, they're always average in some very special way.

Perseverance 238

Remember, as you struggle, and as you grow, that blossoms bloom at the branch's end.

Reading 261

Always keep a good book within reach. Almost certainly it wants to tell you something that will help you.

Self-Reliance

When in times of great need there is a knock on the door of your soul, you are the one who must answer it.

Appendix

A letter I wrote to my sons when they were about to leave for college.

...Never compare your own achievements with others'. You have no control over others' successes or failures. Pay attention only to your own gifts and strive, always, only to do the best with what you have. In some cases it will place you first; in others it will place you last. But in all cases it will fill your spirits and provide you with a contentedness and respect that will last you long after the race is over.

Preface

Every once in a while we stumble upon words that touch us, that resonate with us, that make us re them over and over, and over again. Because we feel them *change* us. Or, at least, because they make us begin to *want to change.* And yet, those same words haunt us days later because we have lost them somewhere in the recesses of our mind. We have forgotten them. We may still recall their essence. We may recall the lesson. But we can't recall the *language* that sent us, momentarily at least, into a world where we felt awe. Which is a world in which we feel awesome.

Instead, we find ourselves in a world of frustration. "What was it," we ask ourselves, "that Emerson said that so encapsulates the value—and pleasure—of knowledge?" "What was it that Mark Twain said about a cat sitting on a hot stove?" "What was it that Abraham Lincoln said he would do for the first 4 hours if he was given 6 hours to chop down a tree?" You knew it once. You read it once. But where? And how many opportunities have you had since, to share it, to delight the minds of others with a neat story, a neat quote, at a perfect moment—only to be silent, searching for the words, and coming up short?

And then there are those other situations where you know that tomorrow a subject will come up. You remember reading somewhere the perfect words related to that subject. But you not only don't remember the words, you don't remember the book you read them in. So much for tomorrow. You had hoped to be quick, and, instead, you were quiet.

Well, hopefully, this book will help you. You may not remember everything, but there will be words that stick with you. And you will be happier for them. I originally published a book entitled, "Words to Remember, Mine and Others." This is a substantially new edition of that book.

My own words are set out in the beginning of each chapter.

Throughout the book, if words are not credited to someone else they are mine.

Enjoy!

Introduction

Let's start with a story, a true one.

Picture the actress Helen Hayes, known as the First Lady of American theatre. She is seated on a train opposite a woman obsessed with her own jewelry, seemingly capable of doing nothing but showing it off. Helen, wearing no jewelry except for her simple wedding band, listened . . . and smiled.

She smiles because she realizes how fortunate she is not to care for *things,* but to have so much, to have gained so much—not materially, but intellectually and emotionally—from reading. In fact, as the lady drones on about her jewelry, Helen recites to herself four simple lines of Emerson that always remind her of all that reading has given her:

> *I am the owner of the sphere*
> *of the seven stars and the solar year*
> *of Caesar's hand and Plato's Brain*
> *of Lord Christ's heart and Shakespeare's strain*

This is the gift of literature. Look at all that is said within these four simple lines. Emerson is describing the knowledge of the world that is available to all of us: Astronomy (the Seven Stars), Time itself (the solar year), History (Caesar's hand), Philosophy (Plato's brain), Religion (Lord Christ's heart) and Literature (Shakespeare's strain). And he is telling us that he has access to all of it—to the world—simply by *reading*.

We might have said, when trying to express the same thoughts, "I love to read. Anything in the world is there for me. . . . the universe and all its glory,('I am the owner of the sphere') the stars, their constellations, the planets, time itself ('of the seven stars and the solar year'), all history ('of Caesar's hand'), the accomplishments and mistakes of mankind, all genius, all philosophy ('and Plato's brain'), all religion and goodness ('of Lord Christ's heart'), and all expression of thoughts that we wish we had had ourselves, or, having recognized them as our own, wish we could have expressed them in those words ('and Shakespeare's strain.')"

Or we might have said it better, as Emerson did.

What I also love about this verse, and great literature generally, is its use of language that forces me to grow. I probably should have known what Emerson meant by "the Seven Stars". I should have known that they refer to the Big Dipper, Ursa Major, because it is made up of seven stars. But I didn't. Instead, I assumed that Emerson meant only that reading gave you access to that body of knowledge commonly referred to as "astronomy". I didn't connect the seven stars to the Big Dipper, though, and I didn't know why he had used that phrase. I do now. Because I looked it up.

This is what great literature—all great reading— does for you: It takes you on a journey you might never have traveled, and leaves treasures along the way, some of which you may not open for years, some of which you may have opened and used the day you found them, some of which will have sat at your feet to this day, which will never be appreciated. It enlarges the possibilities of your life by enlightening you to the lives of others. It forewarns you of losses that you might encounter, and teaches you how to manage them. It emboldens you with stories of others' weaknesses and their perseverance. It reminds you of—or reveals for you—your own potential, and encourages you to own, rightfully so, your own thoughts, made majestic by others' words. And it is so often the missing piece to a puzzle you had not known to exist. It makes you grow.

My father had a photographic memory and a love of poetry, of philosophy and theology. When I was a child he awed my friends and me, and everyone who knew him, with an ability to call to mind from memory poems of Shakespeare, of Tennyson and anyone else whose words and thoughts he loved. I don't have his talent, or his mind. What I have, and I believe it comes from him, is a love of learning, a love of reading, and a love of searching for words that fulfill me as they fulfilled him.

We are searchers in life. We search for things that touch us, that affect us in ways that make us better, whether it be a friend's laughter, a sunset, an achievement, love, or countless other things.

I remember having read a poem when I was working a summer job at Continental Can Company in Milwaukee, Wisconsin (during a break, of course). I loved it. Years later, I tried to recall it, but couldn't remember its title or the name of its author. For years I searched for it but couldn't find it. I could only recall that it described a bird on a limb that gave way, and that the bird was safe because it could fly.

Then, by chance, I happened to pick up a book at a library. I opened it, and there it was—exactly where I had opened the book! That feeling is, for me, what reading gives us. It was like rediscovering an old friend, someone who had been good to me in the past and whose memory always filled me with joy. The poem itself is short, and probably not noteworthy for many. But for me it is, and here it is, that little poem:

Be like the bird who,
Halting in his flight
On limb too slight,
Feels it give way beneath him,
Yet sings,
Knowing he has wings.
Victor Hugo

When I read that poem it empowers me. It helps me "be like the bird". I know I don't have the wings of a bird. I know that if I fall from a limb "too light" I will, in fact, fall.

Why, then, does it empower me, rather than remind me of what powers birds have that I don't? Because I know that I have powers that birds don't have. And the challenges birds may face (limbs too slight, for example) are different than the challenges I most likely will encounter. And the powers that I have to overcome my challenges are no less adequate against those challenges than are the wings of a bird against the challenge of falling to the ground.

I have searched most of my life for words and ideas like these—words that touch me and empower me. They may come to me in the form of a poem, a story, a joke, literally any form. However they come, they make me pause, often in awe of how someone can say so much so well.

Over the years I have written down some of those words. Some are in the form of poems, some in essays, and some in simple quotes. Some are stories, some are jokes. All parts of this collection, though, share one prerequisite: They made me think, and how they made me think made me feel different than I had before I read them, usually better.

Here are many of them. Whether each of them strikes you in the way they have stricken me I can't say, but I am confident that you will find at least some words that will stay with you for the rest of your life, and give you pleasure for just as long.

What I love about the selections in this book is that they inspire my own thought. They make me want to respond, to express myself. They force me—in the happiest sense of that word—to work through what is said, to make certain I understand it, to loll in the beauty of how that thought is expressed and, most importantly, to relate the expression to life as I have experienced it, or how I imagine others have experienced it.

Take, for example, a quote from Goethe:

> *I have come to the frightening conclusion that I am the decisive element. It is my personal approach that creates the climate. It is my daily mood that makes the weather. I possess tremendous power to make life miserable or joyous. I can be a tool of torture or an instrument of inspiration. I can humiliate or humor, hurt or heal. In all situations, it is my response that decides whether a crisis is escalated or de-escalated, and a person is humanized or de-humanized. If we treat people as they are, we make them worse. If we treat people as they ought to be, we help them become what they are capable of becoming.*

What an exhilarating and encouraging, yet frightening, thought . . . that each of us contains within ourselves the ability to make the best of our circumstances, our surroundings, and our lives.

It is more than looking at the bright side of misfortune. It is recognizing that misfortune happens. It is accepting the misfortune that comes into our lives, with the resolve to refocus on the goodness of the balance of our lives. It is to recognize that men are known best not by their experiences, but by their responses to those experiences.

It's even more—It's accepting, and remembering, for better or worse, that we have more control over our circumstances than our circumstances have over us, and we should stand ready to accept the blame or take the credit for what we make of them.

It may not take a genius to realize that our decisions influence our lives. As Robert Louis Stephenson said, "Sooner or later we must all sit down to a banquet of our own consequences." The genius lies in his ability to communicate the thought with words that brighten our own thoughts on the same subject, words that help us think for ourselves.

New ideas and thoughts are typically only repackaged old ideas and thoughts. But when they come back to us in our own packaging they render us new; they change us. And we can feel it.

This isn't a collection or book that you should read from cover to cover, unless that's how you choose to read it. I've broken down my selections into different chapters or themes. That way, if you're in the mood to read about a certain theme you can find it more easily. I have started each category with words of my own, and then set out the words of others that have inspired me throughout my life.

I hope you enjoy . . . and I hope you find some words —at least, *some*—that help you in your life!

Acceptance

When we decide to "accept," a part of us dies, and a part is born.
We need to focus on the newborn.

The good sun rises
and gives us warmth,
in its time—
Do not rush the sun.

Close your eyes and breathe.
Let it be. Let it go. Now.
Acceptance is good.

The irony is that we better our world
when we accept it.
But never confuse acceptance with surrender.
We must continue to move.

If there is a challenge we confront in life every day of our lives, it is the challenge of our discontent, which leads to the challenge of how we respond to it. Remember this: We admire and respect others not because of their experiences, but because of how they have responded to their experiences.

Endless men and women have spent years of their life in prison, yet it is how Nelson Mandela *responded t*o his imprisonment that earns our respect and admiration. It is not for his legendary 1,000 failed-light-bulb-experiments that we honor Thomas Edison, but for his resolve to keep going despite his failures. So too with Walt Disney, Winston Churchill, the Wright brothers, Abraham Lincoln, Emily Dickinson, Theodor Seuss Geisel and many, many more whose failures might easily have stopped them if they had not chosen how best to respond to them.

Whatever it is in life that you're not happy with and that's outside of your control, you have a choice to make: engage in the eternal struggle to make things different, or accept them as they are.

Before you do either, make sure that you've realistically considered whether you have the *ability* to change whatever it is you want changed. No one ever set a goal, or achieved one, while underestimating his abilities and opting to "accept" that he can't accomplish something because it's too difficult.

If there's a secret to the peace "acceptance" gives you, it lies in the fact that you know that you have first given your best efforts. Then, you realize, "it"—whatever it may be that you have "failed" to achieve—is outside of your control. It's time then to pick it up, put it on your "lesson table," get what you can from it, but don't waste your time or ruin your life dwelling on "what might have been."

The great Serenity Prayer captures perfectly the role acceptance should play in our lives.

> *God grant me the serenity*
> *to accept the things I cannot change,*
> *the courage to change the things I can,*
> *and the wisdom to know the difference.*
> The Serenity Prayer (Reinhold Niebuhr)

Take, for example, your worst habit—the habit you wish you had never developed, or the habit you most enjoy that you know strips you of the character you wish you had, undermines your physical health, or contaminates your mind.

Now change it . . . or don't.

Habits belong to us. They are ours. No one has the right (or the ability) to steal them from us, or foist them on us. We reserve that right for ourselves. We are the ones who choose our habits.

So when you're choosing to indulge, or complain about things for which you are responsible, don't even think of the Serenity prayer—You already know "the difference." You've just chosen to ignore it.

You would think it would be simple to "accept" our past mistakes, or whatever it is that would make our lives more joyful, if we could accept what's happened to us in our past. Clearly we can't undo what's been done—We did what we did, said what we said, or had it done or said to us.

So why do we spend so much of the rest of our lives dwelling on the pains of our past, regretting things we can't do anything about, re-living the worst times of our lives over and over, wishing for the impossible—that the past be different?

Whenever we wish that the past were different we have the "wisdom" to understand that we can't change these things. We don't need the "courage" to change them. All we need to do is "accept." And when we do accept, our present days and nights open up to us, making them available for us to fill them with positive thoughts and actions, when previously there was no room for anything but the torment of the past.

And that is the power of acceptance. However much we mourn, however much we regret, however much we cry, or seethe, despair, or wish, our past will not only be unchanged; instead, it will be empowered, pulling us back to those worst times in our lives. Not only that, it will occupy our present time, stripping from it any ability "Now" may have to help us move on, to produce, to use best the only time that serves us well—our Present.

We all have regrets. If we "accept" them, we can turn them from the stumbling blocks they were to the building blocks they should be. They then become responsible not for sadness and sympathy, but for action and resolve . . . and, ultimately, for growth.

My point is that the Serenity Prayer might as well have been called the Wisdom Prayer, the Courage Prayer, or the Acceptance Prayer. In fact, those who seek serenity itself and overlook or minimize the need for their own contributions are unlikely to reap the serenity they seek.

For instance, it is each of us who must decide when to accept the things we "cannot change". That clearly shouldn't be done until we first determine that we can't change those things we wish to change.

And that can't be done until we make our best effort to change them.

The true measure of a happy life begins and ends with our decision to accept into our lives less when we want more, enough when we want more, and,, most importantly, *ourselves* when we want more.

"Happy" may not be the right word. That generally suggests more than an "acceptance" of a situation. But if there's a state just short of happiness—we might call it contentedness—that is the state you will find. And contentedness is really a very comfortable state, one that leaves you very open to the state that shares its longest boundary: Happiness.

One problem with acceptance, though, is that we sometimes associate it with weakness. Ironically, when we accept in accordance with the Serenity Prayer, we don't show weakness; we show a mastery of our mind, and we show that strength that is required of anyone who can say in the face of loss or tragedy, defeat or desire, that we admit that we are not everything, that we can't have everything, and can't do everything . . . and that we have chosen to *live,* rather than lose, our lives.

In a sense, acceptance leads to something even more magical than itself: a redirection. It can be a redirection of our priorities, goals, efforts, thoughts or anything else that needs change for us to progress. It is, then, a beginning, a fresh start in that isolated region of our lives that called for acceptance. And, as with any new beginning, we look to *ourselves t*o take that first step. And with each step that follows, we distance ourselves from all that was so inherently difficult to accept.

Generally, we think of acceptance as a tool for dealing with negative things that already exist in our life, and certainly that is most often the case. Some people have developed the ability, though, to use acceptance for more. They view life with an open mind and "accept" all that comes into their lives, opting to see each new event as something that should be, something that serves a purpose, or something that simply will serve as a guide to our growth as a human being. Not easy, but there's no denying that this practice must make them much more successful in coping with what the rest of us struggle to accept.

In the end, it comes down to this: Each of us should do what each of us can do. And when we've tried, when we've failed—

then, and only then—should we accept and feel the peace of earned serenity.

To let go doesn't mean to stop caring, it means I can't do it for someone else. To let go is not to cut myself off, it's the realization that I can't control another. To let go is not to enable, but to allow learning from natural consequences. To let go is to admit powerlessness, which means the outcome is not in my hands. To let go is not to try to change or blame another, I can only change myself. To let go is not to care for, but to care about. To let go is not to fix, but to be supportive. To let go is not to judge, but to allow another to be a human being. To let go is not to be in the middle arranging all the outcomes, but to allow others to effect their own outcomes. To let go is not to be protective, it is to permit another to face reality. To let go is not to deny, but to accept. To let go is not to nag, scold, or argue, but to search out my own shortcomings and to correct them. To let go is not to adjust everything to my desire, but to take each day as it comes and to cherish the moment. To let go is not to criticize and regulate anyone but to try to become what I dream I can be. To let go is not to regret the past, but to grow and live for the future. To let go is to fear less and love more. Source Unknown

---

I would like to beg you dear Sir, as well as I can, to have patience with everything unresolved in your heart and to try to love the questions themselves as if they were locked rooms or books written in a very foreign language. Don't search for the answers, which could not be given to you now, because you would not be able to live them. And the point is to live everything. Live the questions now. Perhaps then, someday far in the future, you will gradually, without even noticing it, live your way into the answer.

Letters to a Young Poet by Rainer Maria Rilke

We must embrace pain and burn it as fuel for our journey.
 Kenji Miyazawa quote

Each mind has its own method. A true man never acquires after college rules. What you have aggregated in a natural manner surprises and delights when it is produced. For we cannot oversee each other's secret. And hence the differences between men in natural endowment are insignificant in comparison with their common wealth.

Do you think the porter and the cook have no anecdotes, no experiences, no wonders for you? Everybody knows as much as the savant. The walls of rude minds are scrawled all over with facts, with thoughts. They shall one day bring a lantern and read the inscriptions.

Everyman, in the degree in which he has wit and culture, finds his curiosity inflamed concerning the modes of living and thinking of other men, and especially of those classes whose minds have not been subdued by the drill of school education.
 Emerson, Essay on Intellect

You never really understand a person until you consider things from his point of view . . . until you climb into his skin and walk around in it. Harper Lee, To Kill a Mockingbird

---

To offer no resistance to life is to be in a state of grace, ease and lightness. This state is then no longer dependent upon things being in a certain way good or bad.

There are cycles of success, when things come to you and thrive, and cycles of failure when they wither or disintegrate, and you have to let them go in order to make room for new things to arise or for transformation to happen.

If you cling and resist at that point, it means you are refusing to go with the flow of life, and you will suffer. Dissolution is needed for new growth to happen. One cycle cannot exist without the other.
--Eckhart Tolle, The Power of Now

How wild it was, to let it be.

Cheryl Strayed, Brave Enough

For after all, the best thing one can do when it is raining is let it rain.

Henry Wadsworth Longfellow

Most things will be okay eventually, but not everything will be. Sometimes you'll put up a good fight and lose. Sometimes you'll hold on really hard and realize there is no choice but to let go. Acceptance is a small, quiet room.

Cheryl Strayed— Tiny Beautiful Things

Don't surrender all your joy for an idea you used to have about yourself that isn't true anymore.

Cheryl Strayed — Tiny Beautiful Things

"And Lot's wife, of course, was told not to look back where all those people and their homes had been. But she did look back, and I love her for that, because it was so human. So she was turned to a pillar of salt. So it goes. People aren't supposed to look back. I'm certainly not going to do it anymore." – Kurt Vonnegut, Slaughterhouse-Five

Attitude

One blossom alone may suffice to entice.
Bouquets may prove too few.
The difference is never in number.
The difference is in you.

If acceptance is the peacemaker in life, attitude is the gunslinger, the conductor, the creator. It can turn upside down every reality, every emotion, every experience. It moves us into a world of our own where we enjoy, or suffer, its consequences. Our attitudes make our reality, often making what is large, too small, or what is small, too large. No goodness, no evil, no joy or sadness escapes the impact of attitude.

The person thankful that thorns have roses is thankful even though his roses have thorns. In his mind, the rose predominates among insignificant thorns. And with this outlook, not only has he changed the appeal of the rose; he has changed himself. The thorns are of no consequence; thankfulness overwhelms them. Just as true, is that the man who focuses on the thorns will never absorb the wonder of the roses. Each of them lives in different worlds, one with roses, one with thorns.

There is a wonderful story told in the epilogue of the book All Things Shining, by Hubert Dreyfus and Sean Dorrance Kelly. Two students had studied for many years with a wise old master. One day the master said to them, "Students, the time has come for you to go out into the world. Your life will be felicitous if you find in it all things shining."

The students left the master with a mixture of sadness and excitement, and each of them went a separate way. Many years later they met up by chance. They were happy to see one another again, and each was excited to learn how the other's life had gone.

Said the first to the second, glumly, "I have learned to see many shining things in the world, but alas I remain unhappy. For I also find many sad and disappointing things, and I feel I have failed to heed the master's advice. Perhaps I will never be filled with happiness and joy, because I am simply unable to find all things shining."

Said the second to the first, radiant with happiness, "All things are not shining, but all the shining things are."

Each of the students had approached life with a different attitude. One, understanding the master's instructions to mean that we should focus on the "shining things" in our lives; although there clearly are unhappy events in life, we need to focus on what is good in our lives. He did, and his life was a happy one.

The other student misunderstood and thought the master meant that we should somehow see all things in life as shining; that we should see them as good even if they are not. This, of course, was impossible, and the student lived a sad life trying to follow what he thought the master had meant, in all likelihood spending too much of his life focused on the bad things in life, wishing that they were different. That time was time that he could have spent focusing on the best that his life offered.

So one lived with an attitude where he focused on the good, happy parts of his life, and lived well. The other lived with an attitude where he expected all things to be good, and lived a life of disappointment.

For we who love to travel,
to wander, just to roam,
our travels have us love the more

the pillow rest of home.

Who would think that travel
—itself a cherished prize—
would enhance our love for a simple home
by en-light-en-ing our eyes?

There is, of course, no change in home
from our travels far and wide—
The change we feel when we return
Is a change *we've* made inside.

Tomorrow will be a great day for me.
I'm going to practice the piano for two hours, or an hour.
I'm going to read a Great Book, not just a best-seller.
I'm going to start writing a novel (even though I rarely read them.)
I'm going to work hard—at something—and actually accomplish something.
I'm going to volunteer my time for a good cause, right after I do what I should to find a good cause.
I'm going to make a better friend out of a friend by listening, by paying attention to what's going on in his life, and by caring enough for him to know that I care enough.
I'm going to look back on stories I've told, heard or read that have changed my life, if only because I love them.
I'm going to take a hard look at consequences—those difficult ones I deserve and those joyful ones I've earned—and remind myself that now is the time to work on those difficult ones.
I'm going to make a difference in my life, and hope that it translates into a good difference in others' lives.
I'm going to tell one story to a friend, or a stranger, and tell him it's a true story—even if it's not—because it should be true.
I'm going to think of my grandchildren and what their lives would be like if I changed, or didn't, and leave it up to them.

I'm going to eat healthy, and throw out all the brownies but one.
I'm going to find out whether that person who ignores me
doesn't like me, or just thinks I don't like him.
I'm going to surprise myself at some random time tomorrow and
just absorb all the goodness in my life until I find myself saying ,
just under my breath, "Wow!" and then—most important of all—
saying, "Thank you, God!"
I'm going to doubt myself just enough to feel down, and then
talk myself back to confidence, whether or not I've ever been
there, so that I feel the inimitable power of Choice in my life.
I'm going to explain to a good friend why he is such a good
friend.
I'm going to sweep up the dust in my life.
I am going to try to tap into the minds of anyone I have contact
with to find out what they know and understand better than I ever
could—because everyone knows and understands something
better than I ever could.
I'm going to imagine everyone in my world carrying a cross, so I
don't ignore the crosses they carry that I can't see.
I'm going to remind myself that whenever I have no choice but
to "accept the things I cannot change," it might be best to change
myself.
Yes, Tomorrow will be a great day.
It always has been.

Try staring at a window. Not *through* a window, but *at* a
window. Now look through it. Now ask yourself, "Am I focusing
on the things in my life that are most important?" Re-focusing
could make a huge difference.

The difference between living with gratitude, and not, is the
difference between looking through a window, and at one.

There I was just staring at the window. Not *through* the
window, but *at* the window. And then everything changed. It was

all there: the water, the beach, pretty much a panorama of wonder. Just because I changed the way I looked at something.

The progress is made not when you wish for others to change, but when that is the wish you decide to change.

Look For Yourself

[Adapted from story told in the epilogue of the book All Things Shining, by Hubert Dreyfus and Sean Dorrance Kelly, set out earlier.]

The Story

It was their last day. The two students were saying goodbye to their Zen Master, and as they began their life's journey he said to them, "Remember—Always look for your self."

And with that last advice, they parted ways.

Many years later, the two students came across each other, and they were curious to see how each other's lives had evolved.

"I have not led a good life," the first student said.

"I have done just what our master instructed—I have looked out for myself in all parts of my life; I've looked to others for what they might do for me, and cared nothing for what I might do for them; I've helped myself to more and more, before others even had enough; I've lived my life looking out for no one but myself, and our master could not have been more wrong—none of this has fulfilled me.

"But the master didn't actually say, 'Look out for yourself,'" the second student replied.

"He said, 'Look for your self,' and there is a difference."

"I have looked for my self throughout my life," the second student explained.

"I've looked for my self in those who are weak, so that I might better understand their weaknesses, and my own, for I have weaknesses myself.

"I have looked for my self in everyone who has hurt me, for I have hurt others myself, and wish I had not.

"I've looked for my self in those whom I have forgiven and in those who have forgiven me, for we are the same, and forgiveness has given us a peace, and made each of us better.

"I've looked for my self also in those who are better than I am, those who are stronger than I am, and those who are wiser than I am, for in their goodness, in their strength and in their wisdom, I see what I can be.

"Yes, I have looked for my self in every wrong that others commit against me, with the hope that I will understand those who do me wrong—and myself—better.

"And I have looked for my self in every good that others do,
with the hope that I might do such good myself.

"Our Master was right—Look for your self.

Your lessons are in the search."

Patience is a place
where the race is *not* run,
so that we might win it.

I have a pet named "Yesterday" because—what
seems like a lifetime ago—
he used to just bark and chew at my pantlegs,
but today he growls,
and his bite is real, and vicious.

He has changed so much
from what I remember,
and everywhere I go he follows me.

Every day, it seems,
he comes home a little different,
a little meaner, a little more vicious.

The barking and the chewing

I could deal with at the time,
but now I dread his coming home.

Some days I don't recognize him.
Some days I wonder if he's the same little puppy
I used to call "Mistake."
Some days I wonder how this little puppy
could change so much and snarl so often.

And I never expected that he would consume my days.

He needs to be trained.

——————————————————

You have a decision to make.
It is only yours to make.
Today
—at least one chosen moment of today—
may represent the threshold of your future,
and you are as young today
as you will ever be.

On your deathbed *you* will tell your story,
and you will tell it either
as the moments that "happened" to you,
or as the moments that you *created*.

That is the choice you have today—
to let your future just happen to you,
or to go out and make it happen.

Whatever your choice,
it is the small decisions made easily
that will make the difference.

It is in our **struggles** that we **learn** to change, in our **thoughts** *how* we change, but in our **actions** *that* we change.

Our attitudes create our lives. It's not only what we look at, but how we look at it. What we choose to see is what we choose to be.

Who doubts the wisdom or the joy of the child who on Christmas morning ignores the most lavish gifts and plays with the ribbons? When we master the ability first to notice, and then to love, the "ribbons" in our lives, we change, and every "ribbon" changes for us as well.

C.C. Carter has written a poem that wreaks attitude. It's called The Herstory Of My Hips, and in it she talks proudly of her 46 inch hips. She wonders why you might have a problem with them.

"The second largest continent in the world sired these hips
Of course they would be as large –", ending with the lines:

"The oldest civilization on earth gave birth to these hips
Of course they would be as wide."

This is a woman with attitude; not only has she "accepted" the size of her hips, she takes pride in them. You can imagine how her attitude affects the way she walks into a room. This is what attitude is all about. It changes us.

Change of State

When rivers adorn the countryside
or the swallow mends its nest,
when the sky surrounds the setting sun
and God's work is at its best,

when morning warms the mountain's pass
or the snows protect the seed
and the Grizzly bear, or languid lion
remembers her young must feed,

when sunrise warms a winter's day
or a sunset meets the moon,
when an infant takes his first few steps
or sees his first balloon,

when strangers greet us with a smile,
or friendship shows its face,
when sleep permits a lovely dream
or a lady lifts her lace,

when adults recapture a child's mind
or the weak become the tough,
when our minds can master the moment—now—
when now becomes enough,

when we see the glory of what exists,
when we learn to live for "now"
our tomorrows, (but only when they come),
should summon not "woe" but "Wow!"

Yes, when what some may see as common
we can see as great,
we have done all we ever need—
we have changed our state.

Our Truths

Don't ever presume to tell someone
the direction of a river's flow
unless you are standing
on his side of the river.

He will never understand you.

A Child's Promise

Tell me about the river,
how deep, how long, how wide.
Tell me of the child,
of the hope he has inside.
Or walk with me
through desert's death
with only sand ahead,
if instead of hope, a child's heart
is filled with fear and dread.

Blue Days

We are the ones who search for stars
Throughout the sunlit day
dismissing the vast and bluest skies—
our Winter's search for May.

Those others who have trust in night,

who feel it is not far,
seize *from their days* a hold of Heaven,
having trust in the nighttime star.

For them, the night will soon be here,
the skies their starry black.
We discontents wishing only then
to have our Heaven back.

    "I had a good day today. Thank you."
    (A simple prayer of gratitude that always makes a good day
better.)

We define ourselves in youth by the things we do, and in old
age by the things we don't.
Keep doing.

It is the sun that sets
that brings to us,
in time,
the glory of the stars
and their light,

as it is life
that sets on us
that may,
in time,
bring *us* to glory,
and enlighten us.

Think of the sunset,

and let your life set as well . . .
for it will.

Now, look for the light—

It is closer than those stars
that fight the night.

It's helpful to make this connection:
Always wanting more,
makes you feel
as if you always have less.

There are those who think they can, and those who think they
can't. They're both right. Henry Ford

The greatest discovery of my generation is that a human being
can alter his life by altering his attitudes of mind. William
James, Harvard psychologist

He who binds himself to a joy
Does the winged life destroy;
But he who kisses the joy as it flies
Lives in eternity's sunrise.
      William Blake, from The Notebook

You should always be aware that your thought creates your world.

> Ken Keyes, Jr., Handbook to Higher Consciousness

I am thankful that thorns have roses. Unknown

A man's richness is best measured by what he can do without.
Thoreau

The mind is its own place, and itself
Can make a heav'n of hell, a hell of heav'n. John Milton

The voyage of discovery lies not in finding new landscapes, but
in having new eyes. Marcel Proust

It is the privilege of the mind to rescue itself from old age.
Montaigne

If you want to fly, you must think lovely thoughts. James M.
Barrie, (Peter Pan)

Do you prefer that you be right, or that you be happy?
...I am never upset for the reason I think.
...I can elect to change all thoughts that hurt.

> Selections from A Course In Miracles

To see a World in a Grain of Sand,
And a Heaven in a Wild Flower,
Hold Infinity in the palm of your hand,
And Eternity in an hour.   William Blake

You never really understand a person until you consider things from his point of view...until you climb into his skin and walk around in it. Harper Lee, To Kill a Mockingbird

---

Desiderata - by Max Ehrmann

Go placidly amid the noise and the haste and remember what peace there may be in silence.

As far as possible without surrender be on good terms with all persons. Speak your truth quietly and clearly and listen to others, even the dull and ignorant; they too have their story.

Avoid loud and aggressive persons, they are vexations to the spirit. If you compare yourself to others you may be become vain and bitter, for always there will be greater and lesser persons than yourself.

Enjoy your achievements as well as your plans. Keep interested in your career however humble; it is a real possession in the changing fortune of time. Exercise caution in your business affairs, for the world is full of trickery. But let this not blind you from what virtue there is; many persons strive for high ideals, and everywhere life is full of heroism.

Be yourself, especially do not feign affection. Neither be cynical about love; for in the face of all aridity and disenchantment it is as perennial as the grass.

Take kindly the counsel of the years gracefully surrendering the things of youth. Nurture the strength of spirit to shield you in sudden misfortune. But do not distress yourself with imaginings.

Many fears are born of fatigue and loneliness.

Beyond a wholesome discipline, be gentle with yourself. You are a child of the Universe, no less than the trees and the stars; you have right to be here. And whether or not it is clear to you, no doubt the universe is unfolding as it should.

Therefore be at peace with God, whatever you conceive him to be; and whatever your labours and aspirations, in the noisy confusion of life, keep peace with your soul. With all its shams, drudgery and broken dreams, it is still a beautiful world.

Be cheerful. Strive to be happy.

Men are disturbed not by things that happen, but by their opinions of the things that happen.   Epictetus

---

Prayer of an unknown Confederate Soldier

I asked God for Strength, that I might achieve,
I was made weak, that I might learn humbly to obey...
I asked for health, that I might do greater things,
I was given infirmity, that I might do better things...
I asked for riches, that I might be happy,
I was given poverty that I might be wise...
I asked for power, that I might have the praise of men,
I was given weakness, that I might feel the need of God...
I asked for all things, that I might enjoy life,
I was given life, that I might enjoy all things...
I got nothing that I asked for- but everything that I had hoped for.
Almost despite myself, my unspoiled prayers were answered.
I am among all men, most richly blessed.

If you measure your shadow, you will find it no greater than before the victory.
Achidamus to Philip of Macedon

The tragedy of life is not death, but what we let die inside us while we live.
Norman Cousins

People are often unreasonable, illogical, and self-centered;
Forgive them anyway. If you are kind, people may accuse you of selfish, ulterior motives;
Be kind anyway.
If you are successful, you will win some false friends and some true enemies;
Succeed anyway.
If you are honest and frank, people may cheat you;
Be honest and frank anyway.
What you spend years building, someone could destroy overnight;
Build anyway.
If you find serenity and happiness, they may be jealous;
be happy anyway.
The good you do today, people will often forget tomorrow;
Do good anyway.
Give the world the best you have, and it may never be enough;
Give the world the best you've got anyway.
You see, in the final analysis, it is between you and God; it never was between you and them anyway.

Mother Teresa

If what we call evil or torment are only evil or torment insofar as our mental apprehension endows them with those qualities then it lies within our power to change those qualities.
Montaigne

It's not because things are difficult that we don't dare; it's because we don't dare that things are difficult.

Seneque

There is neither happiness nor unhappiness in this world; there is only the comparison of one state with another. Only a man who has felt ultimate despair is capable of feeling ultimate bliss. It is necessary to have wished for death in order to know how good it is to live . . . [U]ntil the day when God will deign to reveal the future to man, all human wisdom is contained in these two words, – "Wait and hope." Monte Cristo, The Count of Monte Cristo, Alexandre Dumas

---

My crown is in my heart, not on my head;
Not decked with diamonds and Indian stones,
Nor to be seen. My crown is called content.
A crown it is that seldom kings enjoy. Henry VI, Part Three, III,. I, 62d

---

There is nothing either good or bad, but thinking makes it so.
Shakespeare, Hamlet, II, ii

Glory be to God for dappled things –
For skies of couple-colour as a brinded cow;
For rose-moles all in stipple upon trout that swim;
Fresh-firecoal chestnut-falls, finches' wings;
Landscape plotted and pieced – fold, fallow, and plough;
And all trades, their gear and tackle and trim.

Pied Beauty, Gerard Manley Hopkins

The basic difference between an ordinary man and a warrior is that a warrior takes everything as a challenge, while an ordinary man takes everything as a blessing or a curse.

Carlos Castenada, The Wheel of Time

"A black belt is just a white belt who never quit."

Unknown

The question isn't
whether you should stay or go.

The question is:
How would your life be transformed if
you chose to love this time with all your
intelligence?

Brave Enough, Cheryl Strayed

For a star to be born, there is one thing that must happen: a
gaseous nebula must collapse.
So collapse.
Crumble.
This is not your destruction.
This is your birth.

Annie Neugebauer

The great stoic metaphor is that we're like dogs leashed to a
powerful chariot. When the chariot begins to move we have two
choices: trot or be dragged. Either way, we go to the same place.
The exact same place. (ie of car is stolen we can complain,
whine and otherwise be dragged, but it won't bring back the car.)

The secret of happiness is to make up our mind to trot; to bring
our thoughts in accord with "nature". "Nature" is God's will, or
destiny, or how things work. A broken mug is "nature".

For after all, the best thing one can do
When it is raining, is to let it rain.

Henry Wadsworth Longfellow
From the Rise, Sarah Lewis and discussion of the value of
surrender (as in Aikido)

When we cannot change our circumstances, we are challenged to
change ourselves. Viktor Frankl

Compare yourself to who you were yesterday, not to who
someone else is today.
Jordan B. Peterson,

12 Rules For Life, An Antidote to Chaos

What you aim at determines what you see.

Jordan B. Peterson, 12 Rules For Life, An Antidote to Chaos

The Zen Buddhists have a word for the beginner's mindset: Shoshin. It's the practice of taking everything you think, know, and believe, and setting it aside, and instead adopting an attitude of openness and eagerness when learning something new.

The Big Book of 30-Day Challenges, by Rosanna Casper

You're more likely to act yourself into feeling, than feeling yourself into action. Harvard psychologist Jerome Bruner

---

Something happened to me at 45 that had a shattering effect on my life . . . I suddenly realized one day that the conductor doesn't make a sound. He depends for his power on his ability to make other people powerful. It had an overwhelming effect . . . I realized my job was to awaken possibility in other people.

--Benjamin Zander, conductor and musical director of the Boston Philharmonic Orchestra and the Boston Philharmonic Youth Orchestra

---

I didn't survive. I prepared."
--Nelson Mandela's answer when Tony Robbins asked him, "Sir, how did you survive all those years in prison."

Character

Listen to the eulogies of the wealthy or the brilliant, the athlete or the skilled, and we may feel unconnected, as if they had talents we simply could not develop.

But hear of the man of character, of the good and difficult choices he made throughout his life, and we realize that it comes to all of us not at birth, but one choice at a time, and that no one has an easier path than another on his way to deserving the good eulogy.

Do not be the one whose strengths make you weaker.

If you find yourself having to choose between your character and your reputation, you're thinking of too many things.

If you come to a fork on your way to the building of your reputation, choose the unfinished, obstacle-ridden, uncleared and narrow path; It is that path that is filled with destinations worth reaching.

To paraphrase Mark Twain, "Every man will yield to temptation. You simply need to know what tempts him." Whether or not that is true, and it's difficult to believe it is not, it is all the more reason why good character fills a eulogy—as well as a life— perhaps better than any other achievement.

Be honest. There is no greater testament to a man's character than his reputation for honesty. More important than testament, is that you will find strength in the truth. Lies can follow you forever, and will. The truth does not follow; it leads you, always, to a more fulfilling and peaceful life.

Long ago, in a little gym,
an empty field, or a pool of water,
our childhood coach taught us
to work, to *enjoy*, to compete, to enjoy *more*,
and to *love.*

He taught us all that our young minds
needed, or could absorb,
about *team work, character, drive, persistence,*
and what it means to be "*heartbroken.*"
He taught us how to lose, and how to win,
how to lead, and how to follow.

And long before other, later, coaches
taught us how to *dream,* how to set goals,
how to make ourselves *better,*
at both our sport and our life,

long before one of those coaches finally
reached into our heart and placed that sport
and all of its precious lessons inside us, for life,

long before any of this,

there was a little town in Hungary
that made the finest

horse carriages in the world, for travel between
Budapest and Vienna—
horse carriages so well made, and so renown,
that they came to be named after that little town in
which they were made.

The name of that little town was KOCS,
and it was pronounced "COACH."

That word—"coach"—evolved to refer not only to the finest
horse carriages in the world,
    but also to other forms of transportation, such as
"stagecoach" and "flying coach."

Ultimately, it evolved to mean this:

*A coach is anything or anyone that moves a valued person
from where he is to where he wants to be.*

If you're a coach, you deserve to know this story. And when
someone calls you "Coach," you need to smile—It's a great
honor to have earned the title of "Coach."

A granddaughter of a great friend of mine is in law school and he
asked me if I could suggest to her 5 ways to achieve a *presence*
in the courtroom. We all know if someone has a commanding
presence, whether in a courtroom or a social gathering, but it's a
little hard to put into words what "presence" is.

So I looked it up. "Presence" is "a person's ability to make his or
her character known to others." Having that in mind, here is what
I wrote to her. And as I look at this list of 5 traits that might
improve one's presence in a courtroom, it occurs to me that they
are suggestions that can just as well apply to life itself. Here they

are:

1.   **Exude Competence.** This is very different from exuding confidence. Confidence is important in that it reflects a belief in yourself, and in your client, that can make you—and your client—more trustworthy, but *Competence* will give you a presence more than anything else. Jurors and judges respect and admire competence. Every word you say will hit more attentive ears . . . because they trust you more. You have shown them that you have worked hard, that you must believe in your client's cause, and that maybe, just maybe, they should believe in it too.

2.   **Be respectful of the court**. That means that you must be respectful of the judge, the jurors, the bailiff and the court reporter. *Everyone.* A side benefit to this is human nature—those to whom you show respect, usually show respect back. You want the jurors to believe you have earned their respect.

3.   **Be respectful, courteous and considerate to your adversaries.** Every moment of the trial, at least one juror is watching everything you do. We win cases because our cases have merit, not because we pretend to be better than our adversaries. In everything you do—even in how you treat you adversary—*be professional.*

4.   **Be polite to *all* witnesses, including the opponent's witnesses.** But maintain control with every question you ask. Politely, but sternly. You are in charge of the courtroom.

5.   **Look everyone in the eyes when you speak to them.** This doesn't mean *staring at people*. It means that when you address a jury, you should keep in mind that there are 12 *individuals*. You are telling each of them a story. You are responding to each nod, each look of confusion, each smile or frown. You are looking one in the eyes, then another, and another. Just as if you were having a conversation. You need to forget you're a lawyer. You have taken on the mantle of teacher—one very attentive, concerned, committed and trustworthy teacher. You're there to help them understand. And

vary the tempo and tone of your talk. You're having an important conversation. They should feel that, just like you do.

You may never shoot a sniper rifle. You may never serve as part of an assault team, or stand security in combat, or board a hostile ship at midnight on the high seas. You may never wear a uniform. You may never even throw a punch in the name of freedom. I'll tell you what, though. Whatever it is that you do, you are making a stand for either mediocrity or excellence.

This is what I learned about being a Navy SEAL. It is all about excellence, and about never giving up on yourself. And that is the red circle I will continue to hold, no matter what. The Making of A Navy Seal, by Brandon Webb

---

[C]haracter too is a process and an unfolding. The man was still in the making . . . . And there were both virtues and faults capable of shrinking or expanding. Middlemarch, George Eliot

---

"I know who I am," said Don Quixote, "and who I may be, if I choose." Don Quixote, Cervantes

---

The true measure of a man is how he treats someone who can do him absolutely no good.   Samuel Johnson

---

Above all, do not lie to yourself. A man who lies to himself and listens to his own lie comes to a point where he does not discern any truth either in himself or anywhere around him, and thus falls into disrespect towards himself and others. Not respecting anyone, he ceases to love, and having no love, he gives himself up to the passions and coarse pleasures, in order to occupy and amuse himself, and in his vices reaches complete bestiality, and it all comes from lying continually to others and to himself.

Zosima speaking to Fyodor about the importance of honesty.
The Brothers Karamazov, by Fyodor Dostoevsky

It is your character, and your character alone, that will make your life happy or unhappy. That is all that really passes for destiny. And you choose it. No one else can give it to you or deny it to you. No rival can steal it from you. And no friend can give it to you. Others can encourage you to make the right choices or discourage you. But you choose.
John McCain, Character is Destiny

It was, he thought, the difference between being dragged into the arena to face a battle to the death and walking into the arena with your head held high. Some people, perhaps, would say that there was little to choose between the two ways, but Dumbledore knew - and so do I, thought Harry, with a rush of fierce pride, and so did my parents - that there was all the difference in the world.

— J.K. Rowling

Willy Loman, Salesman
Arthur miller
(Linda Loman is defending her husband, to her two grown sons)

I don't say he's a great man. Willy Loman never made a lot of money. His name was never in the paper. He's not the finest character that ever lived. But he's a human being, and a terrible thing is happening to him. So attention must be paid He's not to be allowed to fall into his grave like an old dog. Attention,

attention must be finally paid to such a person. You called him crazy... a lot of people think he's lost his - balance. But you don't have to be very smart to know what his trouble is. The man is exhausted....A small man can be just as exhausted as a great man. He works for a company thirty-six years this March opens up unheard-of-territories to their trademark, and now in his old age they take his salary away....For five weeks he's been on straight commission, like a beginner, an unknown!...When he brought them business, when he was young, they were glad to see him. But now his old friends, the old buyers that loved him so and always found some order to hand him in a pinch, they're all dead, retired. He used to be able to make six, seven calls a day in Boston. Now he takes his valises out of the car and puts them back and takes them out again and he['s exhausted. Instead of walking he talks now. He drives seven hundred miles and when he gets there no one knows him any more, no one welcomes him.... How long can that go on? How long? You see what I'm sitting here and waiting for? And you tell me he has no character? The man who never worked a day but for your benefit. When does he get a medal for that?...

(After Willy Loman's suicide, an old business friend speaks to the dead man's sons)

Nobody dast blame this man. You don't understand: Willy was a salesman. And for a salesman, there is no rock bottom to the life. He don't put a bolt to a nut, he don't tell youth law or give you medicine. He's a man way out there in the blue riding on a smile and a shoeshine. And when they start not smiling back, that's an earthquake. And then you get yourself a couple of spots on your hat, and you're finished. Nobody dast blame this man. A salesman is got to dream, boy, it comes with the territory. (From The Death of a Salesman)

Some day, in years to come, you will be wrestling with the great temptation, or trembling under the great sorrow of your life. But the real struggle is here, now, in these quiet weeks. Now it is being decided whether, in the day of your supreme sorrow or temptation, you shall miserably fail or gloriously conquer. Character cannot be made except by a steady, long continued process.

Phillips Brooks

It seems logical that when a person overcomes the seemingly insurmountable we find a trend in his past. Those most able to meet the tests of the greatest sorrows and temptations are those who have demanded the best of themselves in the midst of the many smaller disappointments and urges that confront us regularly.

Sow a thought, reap an act;
Sow an act, reap a habit;
Sow a habit, reap a character;
Sow a character, reap a destiny. Anonymous

"A fight is going on inside me," said an old man to his son. "It is a terrible fight between two wolves. One wolf is evil. He is anger, envy, sorrow, regret, greed, arrogance, self-pity, guilt, resentment, inferiority, lies, false pride, superiority, and ego. The other wolf is good. he is joy, peace, love, hope, serenity, humility, kindness, benevolence, empathy, generosity, truth, compassion, and faith. The same fight is going on inside you."

The son thought about it for a minute and then asked, "Which wolf will win?"

The old man replied simply, "The one you feed.""

— from "Jeremy Fink and The Meaning of Life" by Wendy Mass

Abraham Lincoln On Doing Right

I do the very best I know how - the very best I can; and I mean to keep doing so until the end. If the end brings me out all right, what is said against me won't amount to anything. If the end brings me out wrong, ten angels swearing I was right would make no difference.

Do I contradict myself?
Very well then . . . I contradict myself.
I am large … I contain multitudes.
Walt Whitman "Song of Myself"

So oft it chances in particular men
That through some vicious mole of nature in them
By the o'ergrowth of some complexion
Oft breaking from the pale and force of reason
Or by some habit grown too much: that these men
Carrying, I say, the stamp of one defect
Their virtues else - be they as pure as grace
Shall in the general censure take corruption
From that particular fault. (Hamlet)

It is not the critic who counts; not the man who points out how the strong man stumbles, or where the doer of deeds could have done them better. The credit belongs to the man who is actually in the arena, whose face is marred by dust and sweat and blood; who strives valiantly; who errs, who comes short again and again, because there is no effort without error and shortcoming; but who does actually strive to do the deeds; who knows great enthusiasms, the great devotions; who spends himself in a worthy cause; who at the best knows in the end the triumph of high achievement, and who at the worst, if he fails, at least fails while daring greatly, so that his place shall never be with those cold and timid souls who neither know victory nor defeat.

Theodore Roosevelt

Excellence is an art won by training and habituation. We do not act rightly because we have virtue or excellence, but rather we have those because we have acted rightly. We are what we repeatedly do. Excellence, then, is not an act but a habit.
Aristotle

His hidden meaning lies in our endeavors;
Our valors are our best gods.
Emerson, Self-Reliance

A Good Name
William Shakespeare

Iago. Good name in man and woman, dear my lord,
Is the immediate jewel of their souls:
Who steals my purse steals trash; 'tis something, nothing;
'Twas mine, 'tis his, and has been slave to thousands.
But he that filches from me my good name
Robs me of that which not enriches him
And makes me poor indeed. (From Othello)

My fair cousin; if we are mark'd to die, we are honored by our country in its tragic loss. And if we live, the fewer men, the greater the share of honor. God's will, I pray thee, not one more man. For I am not covetous for gold, nor care I for material flourishments. But if it be a sin to covet honor, I am the most offending soul alive. We few, we happy few, we band of brothers; for he today that sheds his blood with me shall be my brother. (Excerpt from Shakespeare's King Henry V's rallying cry to his weary soldiers before the battle of Agincourt.)

Ultra marathon man, by Dean Karnazes

I remember, for instance, when Justin Caldbeck was a manager during his freshman year. (He later worked his way onto the basketball team and was a senior in our 1999 run to the Final Four.) We were holding a basketball camp and Justin was handing out drinks. He handed me one and, while walking away, I accidentally dropped my cup to the floor. Justin quickly grabbed a towel and ran over to wipe up. "Here, Coach, I'll get that," he said. But I asked him for the towel. "Here, let me have that, Justin," I said. "When you are the CEO of your own company, I want you to remember that you should still clean up your own mess." Then I got down on my hands and knees and cleaned the floor. Coach Mike Krzyzewski, Leading With The Heart

---

This is your first game, my child. I hope you win.
I hope you win for your sake, not mine.
Because winning's nice.
It's a good feeling.
Like the whole world is yours.
But it passes, this feeling.
And what lasts is what you've learned.
And what you learn about is life.
That's what sports is all about. Life.
The whole thing is played out in an afternoon.
The happiness of life.
The miseries.

The joys.
The heartbreaks.
There's not telling what'll turn up.
There's no telling whether they'll toss you out in the first five
minutes or whether you'll stay for the long haul.
There's no telling how you'll do.
You might be a hero or you might be absolutely nothing.
There's just no telling.
Too much depends on chance.
On how the ball bounces.
I'm not talking about the game my child.
I'm talking about life.
But, it's life that the game is all about.
Just as I said.
Because every game is life.
And life is a game.
A serious game.
Dead serious.
But, that's what you do with serious things.
You do your best.
You take what comes.
You take what comes
And you run with it.
Winning is fun.
Sure.
But winning is not the point.
Wanting to win is the point.
Not giving up is the point.
Never being satisfied with what you've done is the point.
Never letting up is the point.
Never letting anyone down is the point.
Play to win.
Sure…
But lose like a champion.
Because it's not winning that counts.
What counts is trying.

Unknown, but found in John Wooden's book, Wooden, A lifetime of Observations and Reflections on and off the court

---

"'Tis not in mortals to command success, but we'll do more . . .we'll deserve it." From Play staged by Washington at Valley Forge about Cato's fight against Julius Caesar's dictatorship (We can't promise achievement but we can become the kind of people who are worthy of achievement.) Eric Greitens

---

Out of every one hundred men, ten shouldn't even be there, eighty are just targets, nine are the real fighters, and we are lucky to have them, for they make the battle. Ah, but the one, one is a warrior, and he will bring the others back.   Heraclitus

---

Among men who rise to fame and leadership two types are recognizable—those who are born with a belief in themselves and those in whom it is a slow growth dependent on actual achievement. To the men of the last type their own success is.a constant surprise, and its fruits the more delicious, yet to be tested cautiously with a haunting sense of doubt whether it is not all a dream. In that doubt lies true modesty, not the sham of insincere self-deprecation but the modesty of "moderation", in the Greek sense. It is poise, not pose. 19-20. [Said about General William Tecumseh Sherman, who sought no acclaim, or office, but simply did his job.]

Ego is the Enemy, by Ryan Holiday

It doesn't interest me what you do for a living. I want to know what you ache for, and if you dare to dream of meeting your heart's longing.

It doesn't interest me how old you are. I want to know if you will risk looking like a fool for love, for your dream, for the adventure of being alive.

It doesn't interest me what planets are squaring your moon. I want to know if you have touched the center of your own sorrow, if you have been opened by life's betrayals or have become shriveled and closed from fear of further pain!I want to know if you can sit with pain, mine or your own, without moving to hide it or fade it, or fix it.

I want to know if you can be with joy, mine or your own, if you can dance with wildness and let the ecstasy fill you to the tips of your fingers and toes without cautioning us to be careful, to be realistic, to remember the limitations of being human.

It doesn't interest me if the story you are telling me is true. I want to know if you can disappoint another to be true to yourself; if you can bear the accusation of betrayal and not betray your own soul; if you can be faithless and therefore trustworthy.

I want to know if you can see beauty even when it's not pretty, every day, and if you can source your own life from its presence. I want to know if you can live with failure, yours and mine, and still stand on the edge of the lake and shout to the silver of the full moon, "Yes!"

It doesn't interest me to know where you live or how much money you have. I want to know if you can get up, after the night of grief and despair, weary and bruised to the bone, and do what needs to be done to feed the children.

It doesn't interest me who you know or how you came to be here. I want to know if you will stand in the center of the fire with me and not shrink back.

It doesn't interest me where or what or with whom you have studied. I want to know what sustains you, from the inside, when all else falls away.

I want to know if you can be alone with yourself and if you truly

like the company you keep in the empty moments.
— Oriah Mountain Dreamer, The Invitation.

I once had a mentor who would often tell me that there has never been a drop of rain that believed it was responsible for the flood.   Go Together, Shola Richards

Choices

No clearer or more well traveled paths exist than those that lead
from our successes or failures back to our choices.

―――――――――――――――――――――

It is in the moments just before our habits begin that we
forge our destiny.

―――――――――――――――――――――

When you look back at the worst decisions you've ever made in
your life and realize that you made each of them, literally, in a
split second, it makes sense to believe that you have plenty of
time left to make up for them.

I hate hearing that it's not the events of life that affect us, that it's
how we respond to the events of life . . . because I know it's
true—and I don't always respond well.

How many times have we been in awe of the disabled child who
perseveres and excels in life, or the bereaved parent of a lost
child who focuses not on his loss but on how he can change the
world so others won't experience what he has, or the blind and
deaf and dumb who communicate and teach us not of their
disappointment and suffering but of their joy and wonder of life.

These examples and so many others teach us that our choices
dispose of, perpetuate, or create our misfortunes. They teach us
also that misfortunes can inspire us to overcome them, to have
empathy for others in dealing with their misfortunes, or simply to
teach the appropriateness of gratitude to the more fortunate.

―――――――――――――――――――――

The father called for his little boy.
The boy came and asked his father why he had called him.

"I just made this mirror, and I thought you might find it

interesting," the father answered.

And so the little boy looked into the mirror.

"Daddy, all I see are pieces of me spread out all over in the mirror!" Why is that?"

"That's because it's a truth mirror," the father said.

"What does that mean?" the little boy asked.

"Well," the father said, "it shows you that there are thousands of little pieces that make up who you are."

"But why are they all spread out?" the boy asked.

"Because it's our job every day to pick out those pieces that we want to become."

Some endeavor forever
heartbreak to instill,
but always,
always,
always . . .
be the good you will.

Resolutions for a new year

I want to attend to those things in my life
I can change for the better.

Those things I can't change, I want to learn to accept.

Above all—having these two simple resolutions in mind—
I want to appreciate the Power of *Now*.

When you find yourself wishing
That you could do better,
You're really wasting time—
It takes time to wish.

---

5 Steps to a Happier You

1. Think before you speak, and say what you mean.
2. Listen closely, and if interpretation is important, ask the source to interpret. Never read minds.
3. Remember that you too say things you don't mean.
You too are misinterpreted everyday.
And you too would appreciate the chance
To clarify, retract, and apologize.
4. Apologize when you've been wrong and hurt someone.
Heartfelt apologies are magical,
And they never start with "If . . ."
5. Accept the apology, if given one.
It will make both lives better.

If we wonder at the outcome of a chess game we need first to look back at the pawns that were lost, and why.
So it is in life—Most of our decisions have consequences, even those we might think of them as relatively unimportant, and should be valued as if the "pawns" might some day prove significant.

Today was a good day
It rained.
My parade was canceled.
I chose to walk alone
and look for others
who ignored the rain,
as I had.

Did you do good yesterday
That made you smile today?
Remember tomorrow, today.

A GOLDEN RETRIEVER'S PHILOSOPHY OF LIFE (OR HOW BEST TO LIVE)

We were lucky to have had "JURY" (our Golden Retriever) in our lives. JU for our son Justin, and RY for our son Ryan.
The name may also have come to mind because we were both lawyers.

He was a wonderful companion, and every day he shared with us A Golden Retriever's Philosophy of Life
(or how best to live.)

Every day.

This is that philosophy:

Make humans happy you are in their life.

Love everyone, be kind, and forgive.

Make eye contact with humans. They love it, and so will you.

Retrieve, to the best of your ability.

Include children, adults, other dogs, even cats—any animals, really—among your friends.

Don't wait for signs of affection from humans—
The affection is there, and it will appear when you do what you do best.

Show your emotions on your face, and with your ears, with your tongue, and with your tail—
you can't imagine how it makes a human feel that you are so excited just to be with him.

Put it behind you . . . never, ever, hold a grudge.

Remember—humans sometimes are dealing with stresses that you can't imagine.
Just be there for them. They will let you know when they're ready.

Take their lead—take note of what humans enjoy. They may have ideas you will love.

Always let humans know that they are "enough," and this is
especially true when they are sick, or tired,
and feel that they can't be enough for anyone.

Finally—and this is a goal worthy of your life—help humans
become more like us . . .
and always lead by example.

Sooner or later, we all have to sit down to a banquet of our
own consequences. Robert Louis Stevenson

Every great mistake has a halfway moment, a split second when
it can be recalled and perhaps remedied. Pearl S. Buck

People who want to grow large in spirit have to pull themselves
together quickly. Mastery shows itself, first, in how you cope
with restricted circumstances.
Goethe, from the poem 'Nature and Art', c. 1800

There was only one catch and that was Catch-22, which specified
that a concern for one's own safety in the face of dangers that
were real and immediate was the process of a rational mind. Orr
was crazy and could be grounded. All he had to do was ask; and
as soon as he did, he would no longer be crazy and would have to
fly more missions. Orr would be crazy to fly more missions and
sane if he didn't but, if he was sane he would have to fly them.
If he flew them he was crazy and didn't have to, but if he didn't
want to he was sane and had to. Yossarian was moved very
deeply by the absolute simplicity of this clause of Catch-22 and
let out a respectful whistle. "That's some catch, that Catch-22,"
he observed. "It's the best there is," Doc Daneeka agreed. The

paradoxical law of "Catch-22"

Catch-22, by Joseph Heller

So many people walk around with a meaningless life. They seem half-asleep, even when they're busy doing things they think are important. This is because they're chasing the wrong things. The way you get meaning into your life is to devote yourself to loving others, devote yourself to your community around you, and devote yourself to creating something that gives you purpose and meaning.

Tuesdays with Morrie: An Old Man, a Young Man, and Life's Greatest Lesson

---

Habit is either the best of servants or the worst of masters.

Nathaniel Emmons

The Road Not Taken, by Robert Frost

Two roads diverged in a yellow wood,
And sorry I could not travel both
And be one traveler, long I stood
And looked down one as far as I could
To where it bent in the undergrowth;

Then took the other, as just as fair,
And having perhaps the better claim,
Because it was grassy and wanted wear;
Though as for that the passing there
Had worn them really about the same,

And both that morning equally lay
In leaves no step had trodden black.
Oh, I kept the first for another day!
Yet knowing how way leads on to way,
I doubted if I should ever come back.

I shall be telling this with a sigh
Somewhere ages and ages hence:
Two roads diverged in a wood, and I--
I took the one less traveled by,
And that has made all the difference.

My experience is what I agree to attend to. William James

Margaret More: Father, that man's bad.
Sir Thomas More: There's no law against that.
William Roper: There is: God's law.
Sir Thomas More: Then God can arrest him.

William Roper: So, now you give the Devil the benefit of law!
Sir Thomas More: Yes! What would you do? Cut a great road
through the law to get after the Devil?
William Roper: Yes, I'd cut down every law in England to do
that!
Sir Thomas More: Oh? And when the last law was down, and the
Devil turned 'round on you, where would you hide, Roper, the
laws all being flat? This country is planted thick with laws, from
coast to coast, Man's laws, not God's! And if you cut them down,
and you're just the man to do it, do you really think you could
stand upright in the winds that would blow then? Yes, I'd give
the Devil benefit of law, for my own safety's sake!

The only thing necessary for the triumph of evil is for good men to do nothing. Edmund Burke

---

Gather ye rose-buds while ye may,
old Time is still a-flying;
And this same flower that smiles today,
tomorrow will be dying.

Robert Herrick

Two natures beat within my breast,
The one is foul, the other blessed.
The one I love, the other I hate;
The one I feed will dominate.
Author Unknown

I went to the woods because I wished to live deliberately, to front only the essential facts of life, so that when I came to die I would not discover that I had not lived.   Henry David Thoreau, Walden

---

If you always do what you always did
you'll always get what you always got. Unknown.

There is a tide in the affairs of men,
Which, taken at the flood, leads on to fortune;
Omitted, all the voyage of their life
Is bound in shallows and in miseries.
On such a full sea are we now afloat;
And we must take the current when it serves,
Or lose our ventures.
Brutus, in Shakespeare's Julius Caesar

He who would learn to fly one day
must first learn to stand and
walk and run and climb and dance;
One cannot fly into flying.
-Friedrich Nietzsche

It is our choices that show what we truly are, far more than our abilities.
J.K. Rowling

Everything I do and say with anyone makes a difference. Gita Bellin

---

You can be obsessed by remorse all your life, not because you chose the wrong thing-- you can always repent, atone : but because you never had the chance to prove to yourself that you would have chosen the right thing.
- Umberto Eco, "Foucault's Pendulum"

Give me six hours to chop down a tree and I'll spend the first four sharpening the axe. Abraham Lincoln

---

"I didn't survive. I prepared." Nelson Mandela's answer when Tony Robbins asked him, "Sir, how did you survive all those years in prison."

Between stimulus and response there is a space. In that space is our power to choose our response. In our response lies our growth and our freedom. Victor E. Frankl

---

"You will learn a lot about yourself if you stretch in the direction of goodness, of bigness, of kindness, of forgiveness, of emotional bravery. Be a warrior for love."

Cheryl Strayed— Tiny Beautiful Things

Good things only happen when you're in motion. Dan Sullivan (entrepreneurial coach)

Do what is right. Let the consequences follow. Unknown

Only God can give us credit for the unkind words we did not speak. Rabbi Kushner

Compassion

Every teardrop has a story it shares
only with the one who sheds it.

"Compassionate" is a good word, but it should be a verb.

The greatest danger of compassion is that it will make the
compassionate feel well enough to believe that they need to do
nothing more.]

Let others' compassion for us never lessen our own
determination, our own drive, our own resolve—our own
actions— to become the best we can become.

We all search for the stones to build the castles of our lives.

We may not see the others' castles.

Some may not yet even have found their stones
to begin the work that must be done.

But their dreams, to them, are just as our dreams are to us.

We need to remember this.

Always.

THE WHOLE MAN

I knew him before
his heart was worn,
before his losses came.

I knew him proud, a loving man,
before his acts of shame.

I knew him loud and laughing too,
children at his knee.
I knew him kind and simple,
no different him from me.

I knew him incomplete, of course;
It's how we know all men.
Another piece, from humankind,
The difference: now and then.

Where is my friend
whose heart was large,
who lived a life of love?
Where the children, the chatter too?
Has a hawk replaced the dove?

There, just there—where found before,
beyond the bough . . .
 its tree,
there . . . yes, there,
if I would care,
as if he
were simply me.

If you can be right today without making someone else feel
they've been wrong, good for you—One day that person may

dare to try to be right again.

Mabel Collins, Light on the Path:

Kill out all sense of separateness. Do not fancy you can stand aside from the bad man or the foolish man. They are yourself, though in a less degree than your friend or your master. But if you allow the idea of separateness from any evil thing or person to grow up within you, by doing so you create karma which will bind you to that thing or person till your soul recognizes that it cannot be isolated. Remember that the sin and the shame of the world are your sin and shame; for you are part of it; your karma is inextricably interwoven with the great karma. And before you can attain knowledge you must have passed though all places, foul and clean alike. Therefore, remember that the soiled garment you shrink from touching may have been yours yesterday, may be yours tomorrow. And if you turn with horror from it, when it is flung upon your shoulders, it will cling more closely to you. The self-righteous man makes for himself a bed of mire. Abstain because it is right to abstain—not that you yourself shall be kept clean.

In Germany they came first for the Communists, and I didn't speak up because I wasn't a Communist. Then they came for the Jews, and I didn't speak up because I wasn't a Jew. Then they came for the trade unionists, and I didn't speak up because I wasn't a trade unionist. Then they came for the Catholics, and I didn't speak up because I was a Protestant. Then they came for me, and by that time no one was left to speak up.

Martin Niemoeller, German Lutheran Pastor

No man is an Iland, intire of it selfe; every man is a peece of the Continent, a part of the maine; if a Clod bee washed away by thae Sea, Europe is the lesse, as well as if a Promontorie were, as well as if a Mannor of thy friends or of thine owne were; any man's death diminishes me, because I am involved in Mankinde; and therefore never send to know for whom the bell tolls; it tolls for thee.

(From John Donne's The Tolling Bell- A Devotion)

If I can stop one heart from breaking,
I shall not live in vain:
If I can ease one life the aching
Or cool one pain,
Or help one fainting Robin
Unto his nest again,
I shall not live in vain. Emily Dickenson

He jests at scars that never felt a wound. Romeo and Juliet, II, ii, 1

Be thankful when you come across someone who is scarred; he will understand you, or help you better understand yourself.

Our human compassion binds us the one to the other - not in pity or patronizingly, but as human beings who have learnt how to turn our common suffering into hope for the future. Nelson Mandela

---

Do not believe that he who seeks to comfort you lives untroubled among the simple and quiet words that sometimes do you good. His life has much difficulty and sadness and remains far behind yours. Were it otherwise he would never have been able to find those words.

Rainer Marie Wilke

A heart is not judged by how much you love; but by how much you are loved by others. – L. Frank Baum, The Wonderful Wizard of Oz

---

"It matters very little whether your judgments of people are true or untrue, and very much whether they are kind or unkind."

Churchill, The Power of Words, by Martin Gilbert, in which Churchill quoted John Ruskin, an English author, poet, artist and social and art critic.

Courage

When you start to sweat, when your body shakes,
when your heart pounds,
when every part of you wishes you were somewhere else,
look out—
Courage has a chance to be born.

For every thousand "confident" people we see,

there is only one who is truly confident

(and that one may simply be oblivious.)

The others are courageous,

and fight through every fear they have

to become better.

Man cannot discover new oceans until he has courage to lose
sight of the shore. Unknown

A ship is safe in harbor, but that's not what ships are for.

William G.T. Shedd

Out on the edge you see all kinds of things you can't see from
the center. Big, undreamed-of things—the people on the edge see
them first. Kurt Vonnegut (from "Tools of Titans by Tim Ferriss)

The most courageous act is still to think for yourself. Edward De Bono

---

Come to the edge, he said.
They said: we are afraid.
Come to the edge, he said.
They came.
He pushed them . . . and they flew. Guillaume Apollinaire

He wishes that he, too, had a wound, a red badge of courage.
Stephen Crane

> Lucio: Our doubts are traitors
> And make us lose the good we oft might win
> By fearing to attempt. Shakespeare, Measure for Measure

While preparing to invade Sicily in 1943, Gen. George Patton issued a list of twenty-seven tactical adages to his commanders. One of them was this:

> Never take counsel of your fears.

> From Bill O'Reilly's A Bold Fresh Piece of Humanity

"It's just like bull riding," said the rodeo champion Ty Murray about an art he was trying to master. "You're never quite ready. It just becomes your turn." (From Dancing on the Head of a Pen" by Robert Benson)

Patience is not very different from courage. It just takes longer.
James Richardson

Walk without a stick
into the darkest
woods.

Brave Enough, Cheryl Strayed

The unifying theme is resilience and faith. The unifying theme is being a warrior and a mother-fucker. It is not fragility. It's strength. It's nerve. And, "if your Nerve deny you—," as Emily Dickinson wrote, "Go above your Nerve."

When a caterpillar enters the cocoon, it turns completely to liquid before the butterfly-to-be begins to constellate. You don't get to retain a few fat little caterpillar legs until you grow an elegant butterfly leg or two. You don't get to hold onto our caterpillar brain while you sprout a wing or antenna. You turn to mush.

Kim Rosen, Saved By a Poem

"I wanted you to see what real courage is, instead of getting the idea that courage is a man with a gun in his hand. It's when you know you're licked before you begin, but you begin anyway and you see it through no matter what." – Harper Lee, To Kill a Mockingbird

---

Long ago, I learned how to be brave, how to go forward always.

-Homer, The Iliad

Out on the edge you see all kinds of things you can't see from the center. Big, undreamed-of things—the people on the edge see them first.   Kurt Vonnegut

---

...

Faith

Miracles

Don't be the unhappy sceptic who looks only
for walking-on-water miracles, and sees none.

Look to the water itself
—the oceans, the lakes, the ponds, rivers and streams—
and tell me you see no miracles.

Is not the Whale a miracle? Or the Walleye?
Or the Shark, the Octopus, the Salmon or Sailfish,
or any other of those limitless creatures
nourished by water—including yourself?

Save for faith those miracles you cannot see,
and open your eyes to the world of miracles you can see,
that you may also some day see
the miracle of the man walking on water.

Take heart in Einstein's mind.
Many of his teachings we can never understand.
Many are counter to what we see as truth.
Many of them were doubted before him.
Yet, his teachings have been proven true.
Why should we insist
on understanding God's mysteries
when we can't even understand Einstein's?

Believing in God without believing in yourself is . . . interesting.
What is it about God that you believe?

The difference between hope and faith is the difference between
house and home.

There is a new rule for expedited access to Heaven: If you
never criticize another for sins that are less than your own,
you're in—automatically.

I can have faith in a friend, or a dog, based on past experience. It
seems, however, that my faith in God, must be independent of
experience, and often despite it.

I wrote this poem after my brother's death, having witnessed my
parents' grief.

If I sit alone today,
If I force myself to pray,
Will someone answer, will someone know:
Why did you come?
Why did you go?

And why does my mind each hour, each day,
Search for the answers, long for the way
To feed you and wash you and watch while you play
To hold you—to keep you—
For just one more day?

Why when I know your soul is with Him
Does each part of me ache
From my soul to my limb?

Why each day as I sit in this place
Do my mind and my heart
Burn with your face?

Give me the faith to make the demand,
to scream to the sky,
"Give me his hand!"

That's what I pray, this is my part,
To live each day
with you in my heart,

to trust in the One
who gave you to me
as I trust in the tides
of the consistent sea.

I miss you and love you;
you are my son.
Someday we will touch—
God's will be done.

The way it *is,*
is to make us stronger.

The Album of Life

We may write our names in albums,
     We may trace them in the sands,
Or chisel them in marble,
     With a firm and skillful hand.
But the pages soon are sullied.
     Soon each name will fade away.

Every monument will perish
     Like all earthly hopes away.
But dear friend there is an album
     Full of leaves of snowy white
Where no name is ever tarnished.
     But forever pure and bright
In that "Book of Life" God's Album
     May our names be hewed with care,
And all who here have written
     Write their names forever there.

          Gordon L. Hiley
          Abergavenny (Wales)
          January 1st '08 (1908)

Doubt is a pain too lonely to know that faith is his twin brother. Kahil Gibran, The Prophet

---

What in me is dark
Illumine, what is low raise and support;
That to the height of this great argument
I may assert Eternal Providence,
And justify the ways of God to men.

Paradise Lost, John Milton

Nor do I seek to understand that I may believe, but I believe that I may understand. For this too I believe, that unless I first believe, I shall not understand. St. Anselm, Archbishop of Canterbury, Proslogion

---

The Final Analysis

People are often unreasonable, illogical and self-centered;
Forgive them anyway.
If you are kind, people may accuse you of selfish, ulterior
motives;
Be kind anyway.
If you are successful, you will win some false friends and some
true enemies;
Succeed anyway.
If you are honest and frank, people may cheat you;
Be honest and frank anyway.
What you spend years building, someone may destroy overnight;
Build anyway.
If you find serenity and happiness, they may be jealous;
Be happy anyway.
The good you do today, people will often forget tomorrow;
Do good anyway.
Give the world the best you have, and it may never be enough;
Give the world the best you've got anyway.
You see, in the final analysis, it is all between you and God;
It was never between you and them anyway.

Mother Theresa of Calcutta

"A Parable of Immortality" by Henry Van Dyke

I am standing upon the sea shore.
A ship at my side spreads her white sails to the morning breeze
and starts for the blue ocean.
She is an object of beauty and strength
And I stand and watch her until at length she hangs
like a speck of white cloud

just where the sea and sky come to mingle with each other.

Then someone at my side says;
"There, she is gone! "
"Gone where? "
Gone from my sight . . . that is all.
She is just as large in mast and hull and spar
as she was when she left my side
and she is just as able to bear her load of living freight
to her destined port.

Her diminished size is in me, not in her.
And just at that moment
when someone at my side says,
"There, she is gone! "
There are other eyes watching her
and other voices ready to take up the glad shout,
"Here she comes! "

And that is dying.
                    Henry Van Dyke

I know God won't give me anything I can't handle. I just wish he didn't trust me so much.

    Mother Teresa

Met a man today. Man I had seen many times before. Just sitting. With his legs crossed, hands knotted together, head hanging, hat down, and collar up. A daily fixture on the stone bench across from the children's fountain on the town green. Asleep, I think. But his lips are moving - very carefully moving. An ordinary average-middle kind of man. Size, age, clothes, condition - all ordinary average-middle. From one to two each day he sat - undisturbed by dogs, children, buses, laughter, rain, or cold. He sat. Saying something to himself, maybe. Daily.

So I asked him. One day I had to ask him. Asked him was he all right (which meant, "what's going on, buddy?")
And you know what he said? Said he was praying. Praying. Not that praying is so strange, but he said he was praying the alphabet. Just reciting the alphabet over and over for an hour each day, leaving it to Almighty God to arrange the letters into the proper words of a proper prayer. What was missing in words, he said, he made up for in fervor. He figured God could handle it and would understand.

Story of a man who prayed fervently, just reciting the alphabet, leaving it to God to arrange the letters into words of a proper prayer. What was missing in words, he said, he made up for in fervor. He figured God could handle it and would understand.

Robert Fulgham (his own)

We Don't Stand

We don't stand at your grave and weep.
You are not there. You do not sleep.
You are a thousand winds that blow.
You are the diamond glints on snow.
You are the sunlight on ripened grain.
You are the gentle autumn rain.
When we awaken in the morning's hush,
You are the swift uplifting rush
Of quiet birds in circling flight.
You are the soft star that shines at night.
We don't stand at your grave and cry.
You are not there. You did not die.

Anonymous [adapted]

Footprints

 One night a man had a dream. He dreamed he was walking
along the beach with the Lord. Across the sky flashed scenes
from his life. For each scene he noticed two sets of footprints in
the sand; one belonged to him, and the other to the Lord. When
the last scene of his life flashed before him, he looked back at the
footprints in the sand. he noticed that many times along the path
of his life there was only one set of footprints. He also noticed
that it happened at the very lowest and saddest times in his life.
This really bothered him and he questioned the Lord about it.
"Lord, you said that once I decided to follow you, you'd walk
with me all the way. But I have noticed that at the worst times in
my life, there is only one set of footprints. How could you leave
me when I needed you the most?"

  The Lord replied " My precious, precious child, I love you and
would never leave you. During your times of suffering and when
you see only one set of footprints, it was then that I carried you."

[When someone believes this—that they are never without God's
care and that His help will show itself in the worst of times—he
will have the strength to withstand more than the strongest who
believes he fights alone.]

The LORD is my shepherd; I shall not want.
He maketh me to lie down in green pastures: he leadeth me
beside the still waters.
He restoreth my soul: he leadeth me in the paths of righteousness
for his name's sake.
Yea, though I walk through the valley of the shadow of death, I
will fear no evil: for thou art with me; thy rod and thy staff they

comfort me.

Thou preparest a table before me in the presence of mine enemies: thou anointest my head with oil; my cup runneth over. Surely goodness and mercy shall follow me all the days of my life: and I will dwell in the house of the LORD forever.

[Those who recognize that God is with them, that they are never alone, will feel the green pastures and still waters even in the midst of life's worst winds. Oh, if we could love ourselves and believe in ourselves as if God were in us—not only with us, but a part of us—fear would not exist.]

The Tiger
William Blake
 Tiger! Tiger! Burning bright
In the forests of the night

What immortal hand or eye
Could frame thy fearful symmetry?

In what distant deeps or skies
Burnt the fire of thine eyes?
On what wings dare he aspire?
What the hand dare seize the fire?

And what shoulder, and what art,
Could twist the sinews of thy heart?
And when thy heart began to beat,
What dread hand? And what dread feet?

What the hammer? What the chain?
In what furnace was thy brain?
What the anvil? what dread grasp
Dare its deadly terrors clasp?

When the stars threw down their spears,
And watered heaven with their tears,
Did he smile his work to see?
Did he who made the Lamb make thee?

Tiger! Tiger! burning bright
In the forests of the night,
What immortal hand or eye
Dare frame thy fearful symmetry?

I never saw a moor,
I never saw the sea;
Yet know I how the heather looks,
And what a wave must be.

I never spoke with God,
Nor visited in Heaven;
Yet certain am I of the spot
As if the chart were given.   Emily Dickinson

The Brain -- is wider than the Sky --
For -- put them side by side --
The one the other will contain
With ease -- and You -- beside –
The Brain is deeper than the sea --
For -- hold them -- Blue to Blue --
The one the other will absorb --
As Sponges -- Buckets -- do --

The Brain is just the weight of God --
For -- Heft them -- Pound for Pound --
And they will differ -- if they do --
As Syllable from Sound --
Emily Dickinson

Ask, and it shall be given you;
Seek, and ye shall find;
Knock and it shall be opened unto you;
for everyone that asketh receiveth;
And he that seeketh findeth;
And to him that knocketh it shall be opened. Jesus of Nazareth

---

I have observed the power of the watermelon seed. It has the
power of drawing from the ground and through itself 200,000
times its weight. When you can tell me how it takes this material
and out of it colors an outside surface beyond the imitation of art,
and then forms inside of it a white rind and within that again a
red heart, thickly inlaid with black seeds, each one of which in
turn is capable of drawing through itself 200,00 times its weight-
when you can explain to me the mystery of a watermelon, you
can ask me to explain the mystery of God.

Williams Jennings Bryan

Amazing grace! How sweet the sound
That saved a wretch like me!
I once was lost, but now am found,
Was blind, but now I see.

Through many dangers, toils, and snares,
I have already come:
'Tis grace has brought me safe thus far,
And grace will lead me home.
- - John Newton, "Amazing Grace"

The search for the exotic, the strange, the unusual, the
uncommon has often taken the form of pilgrimages, of turning
away from the world, the "Journey to the East", to another

country or to a different Religion. The great lesson from the true mystics, from the Zen monks, and now also from the Humanistic and Transpersonal psychologists – that the sacred is in the ordinary, that it is to be found in one's daily life, in one's neighbors, friends, and family, in one's backyard, and that travel may be a flight from confronting the sacred – this lesson can be easily lost. To be looking elsewhere for miracles is to me a sure sign of ignorance that everything is a miracle.

Abraham H. Maslow (from Mountains are Mountains and Rivers are Rivers, edited by Ilana Rabinowitz)

If someone prays for patience, do you think God gives them patience? Or does He give them the opportunity to be patient? If they pray for courage, does God give them courage or does He give them the opportunity to be courageous? If someone prayed for their family to be closer, do you think God zaps them with warm fuzzy feelings? Or does He give them opportunities to love each other?

Morgan Freeman in Evan Almighty

I asked God for strength, that I might achieve.
I was made weak, that I might learn humbly to obey.

I asked for health, that I might do great things.
I was given infirmity, that I might do better things.

I asked for riches, that I might be happy.
I was given poverty, that I might become wise.

I asked for power, that I might have the praise of men.
I was given weakness, that I might feel the need for God.

I asked for all things, that I might enjoy life.
I was given Life, that I might enjoy all things.

I got nothing that I asked for, but everything I had hoped for.

Almost despite myself, my unspoken prayers and true needs were fulfilled.

I am, among all men, most richly blessed.

Unknown Civil War Veteran

"Listen, Sam, if it was nature, nobody wouldn't have tuh look out for babies touchin' stoves, would they? 'Cause dey just naturally wouldn't touch it. But dey sho will. So it's caution."

"Naw it ain't, it's nature, cause nature makes caution. It's de strongest thing dat God ever made, now. Fact is it's de onliest thing God ever made. He made nature and nature made everything else."

Zora Neale Hurston, Their Eyes Were Watching God

An Epilogue
John Masefield

I have seen flowers come in stony places
And kind things done by men with ugly faces.
And the gold cup won by the worst horse at the races.
So I trust. too.

Forgiveness

Too much emphasis is given
to what precedes an act of forgiveness.
Its magic is in what follows it.

At one time or another, I think I've forgiven everyone I *like*.

Now comes the hard part.

Actually, now comes forgiveness.

It's not meant to be easy.
It's meant to be *good*.

They were both judges, after all,
and a choice had to be made.

One judge was a pillar of the community.
A good man. Far better than most.
A life unmarred by sin or scandal (seemingly at least.)

The other was known as much for his past mistakes
as for the fact that he overcame them,
helped others overcome theirs
(because he understood how and why they came to make them)
and who ultimately had achieved the status of judge.

"Which one," the client was asked, "would you like as your judge?"

"I would like the judge who has made mistakes himself, and
remembered them,"
 the client answered,
 "and who believes in redemption, having found it him self."

"But what of the other judge?" his lawyer asked.
"He's a good man and has lived a good life.
Surely, he would be forgiving."

"That may be," the client responded, "because good men
forgive,
and if he hasn't sinned, he clearly is a good man.
But it isn't sin or innocence that leads to forgiveness.
It's the remembrance of our own worst sins that leads us
to forgive."

"Let me be judged by the sinner who remembers."

Before we tie the well-worn noose,
yet again, for another's use,

and before we choose to render blame,
to destroy another's hard-earned name,

we need to take a closer look
at the many chapters in *our* long book.

for one by one, each page—if read—
will show us change *we* need, instead.

For if we find fault in another's slate,
trust that we might find fault in ours as great.

5 Steps to a Happier You

1. Think before you speak, and say what you mean.
2. Listen closely, and if interpretation is important, ask the source to interpret.
3. Remember that you too say things you don't mean. You too are misinterpreted everyday. And you too would appreciate the chance to clarify, retract, and apologize.
4. Apologize when you've been wrong and hurt someone. A heartfelt apology is magical, and they never start with "If . . ."
5. Accept the apology, if given one. It will make both lives better.

I believe I deserve forgiveness for the worst of me because I know the best of me. Never stop looking for the best in others, and you will forgive them as well.

That same sensation of rebirth applies as well when we choose to forgive others. Why is it so difficult to comprehend that when we carry hatred or revenge within us we make it a part of us?

Those who choose not to forgive, imagining that they retain control, should realize that they have controlled only the positioning of their disabling thoughts of hatred, resentment, hurt or vengeance to the beginning, middle or end of their days, while those who have forgiven abandon all control of those wearying thoughts, allowing those thoughts to leave their minds, and lives, entirely.

As long as you harbor resentment, though you claim to have forgiven, you steal from yourself precious space and limit the haven you have left, making it more difficult for joy-bearing vessels to enter.

Forgiveness is the great gift of pardoning a life sentence, for two.

I have a pet named "Yesterday" because, what seems like a lifetime ago,
   he used to just bark and chew at my pantlegs,
   but today he growls, and his bite is real, and vicious.
   He has changed so much from what I remember,
   and everywhere I go he follows me.
   Every day, it seems, he comes home a little different,
   a little meaner, a little more vicious.
   The barking and the chewing I could deal with at the time,
   but now I dread his coming home.
   Some days I don't recognize him.
   Some days I wonder if he's the same little puppy I used to call "Mistake."
   Some days I wonder how this little puppy could change so much and snarl so often.
   And I never expected that he would consume the days of my future.
   He needs to be trained.

A Choice

I am the one who
will choose to forgive,
for I am the one
who chooses to live.

Let him be the one
who holds to despise
and forfeit not one,
but two lonely lives.

Peace cannot come
to the warrior bent
on constant review
of harm once sent,

of arrows let loose
in uglier times,
of words transformed
into uglier crimes.

He must set down his bow,
hold out his hand,
trust in this deed
that he will withstand

all trouble, all pain,
that chance may repeat
in hope that two lives
revenge will not cheat.

Forgiveness doesn't just sit there like a pretty
boy in a bar.
Forgiveness is the old fat guy you have to
haul up the hill.

Brave Enough, Cheryl Strayed

___

You will not be punished for your anger, you will be punished by
your anger. – Buddha

___

A memory is a complicated thing, a relative to truth, but not its
twin. Barbara Kingsolver

___

Forgiveness recognizes
        what you thought
                your brother did to you
has not occurred.
"A Course in Miracles: Workbook for Students--What is
Forgiveness?"

___

Every saint has a past and
Every sinner has a future. 16th century poet

___

There is only one courage and that is the courage to go on dying
to the past, not to collect it, not to accumulate it, not to cling to it.
We all cling to the past, and because we cling to the past we
become unavailable to the present.

Bhagwan Shree Rajneesh, Walking in Zen, Sitting in Zen

___

You make yourself and others suffer just as much when you take offense as when you give offense. Ken Keyes, Jr. Handbook to Higher Consciousness

---

Forgiveness is not always easy. At times, it feels more painful than the wound we suffered, to forgive the one that inflicted it. And yet, there is no peace without forgiveness.

A COURSE IN MIRACLES

Clara Barton, founder of the Red Cross, who never bore grudges, was once reminded by a friend of a wrong done to her some years earlier. "No, " replied Clara, "I distinctly remember forgetting that."

If you would learn the secret of right relations look only for the divine in people and things, and leave all the rest to God. J. Allen Boone, Kinship with All Life

---

Defining the Problem, Wendy Cope

I can't forgive you. Even if I could
You wouldn't pardon me for seeing through you.
And yet I cannot cure myself of love
For what I thought you were before I knew you.

I wondered if that was how forgiveness budded; not with the fanfare of epiphany, but with pain gathering its things, packing up, and slipping away unannounced in the middle of the night.
—Khaled Hosseini, The Kite Runner

"Going back to a troubled past is like putting your hand in a fire, pulling it out because it burns, and then putting it back in so it can heal." Sydney Banks, quoted in Path of No Resistance, by Garrett Kramer

---

It's been said that Forgiveness is to give up all hope for a better past. In other words, to forgive means to give up your desire for power over what you can't control. Resilient people know how to focus their power. And although the past is outside your power, how you live today and how you live tomorrow are still yours to control Resilience, Eric Greitens

---

"He who bears a grudge acts like one who, having cut one hand while handling a knife, avenges himself by stabbing his other hand." Talmud

---

Making the point that it's important to encounter people in a number of different settings if a judgment about them is to be of any consequence, the author of "Mindware, Tools for smart Thinking," by Richard NIsbett, quotes Lincoln: "I don't like that man. I must get to know him better." (And Nesbitt adds "Vary the circumstances of the encounters as much as possible.")

"To forgive is to set a prisoner free and discover that the prisoner was you." Lewis Smedes, From Anne Lamott's book Small Victories

---

Forgiveness is the fragrance that the violet sheds, on the heel that has crushed it. Mark Twain

---

No I didn't forgive you
Out of love

Mercy or sympathy
I forgave because
I knew I would
Need to be forgiven
By someone like me

And if I kept my forgiveness
To myself
In the future
That someone like me
Would also keep
Their forgiveness
And it would kill me

yesterday I was the moon, by noor unnahar

The way you see someone is the way you treat them and the way you treat them is who they become.   Goethe

---

Legendary basketball coaches Bobby Knight and Mike Krzyzewski had not spoken in 9 years. After Coach K was elected to the Hall of fame, he called Knight:

"Coach, I've been elected to the hall of fame. I really don't care what you're mad at me about or what I'm mad at you about, but neither of us is getting any younger and this needs to stop. If I hadn't played for you and coached for you, I wouldn't be going into the Hall of Fame. There's no one other than you who should introduce me at the induction ceremony."

"Mike," Knight said, "I'd be honored." The Legend's Club, John Feinstein

The Power of Forgiveness:
The ship releases its anchor not for the anchor's benefit, but for the ship.
(From The Four Doors, A Guide to Joy, Freedom, and a meaningful life)

Friendship

Friendships more rarely break, than whither from neglect.
Attend to a friend.

Whenever you're feeling down, help a friend up.

Repeat, if necessary.

There is a reason why we use the phrase "making friends."
Whatever ingredients sit on the counter will . . . sit on the
counter, until your work begins.

I wrote this poem to honor a friend who had a hard time
committing to anything, and would always respond to invitations
with the words, "I'll be there (smiling) . . . if I can make it."

If I can make it

"I'll be there...", he'll say,
as if he means it,
with a smile,
a great smile that wraps around his face
and frames a pair of eyes that make you
absolutely believe him

and make you feel that he really will be there,
that your invitation is important to him
because he likes you,

because you truly are a valued friend,
because he wants to be there
with you

more, really, than anything else,
and will be—short of an emergency—
and so it takes you by surprise
when
just at the end,
just before you leave him,
just when you're feeling that special bond,
happy that he's as happy as you are,
he adds
—with eyes you've come to love,
but not believe—
". . . if I can make it."

New Friends

Tomorrow I will meet you,
I promise,
with the warmth of the sun
on our faces,
for today is too warm, I am sorry.
But tomorrow I am free,
free to enjoy your company,
to catch up on old times,
to explain, I hope,
why I could not meet yesterday
or last week,
and to show you my pictures,
pictures of my new friends,
friends I met last week
In the bar,
and the pictures of us when we got together
last year.

It's a bar I only discovered last
month, filled with new faces,
pretty faces, happy, "glad-to-see-you"
kind of people, so far at least
they seem to be.
I told them about you,
how long we'd been friends,
how you've always been there for me,
the great talks we've shared,
how we used to be able to get together more often,
how you joke that we just need to make time
to be with each other,
that life is short.
They said I was lucky to have
You as a friend. I agreed.
I would have
told them more about you but
the karaoke started again
and we had to place the last order of the night.
Wish you'd been there.
In fact, about tomorrow,
why don't you just join me and my new friends
at the bar . . . I bet they buy you a drink.

Message From A Friend

The years have passed,
their glory too,
to an end we could not see,
for when we met
and shared our souls
bliss seemed our destiny.

But age and difference
work their toll
when friends rely on past,

for friendship needs rekindling,
if friendship is to last.

It's not enough to laugh and smile,
to enjoy a summer breeze;
a friend must listen, share and stand
through the coldest winter freeze.

Cold it is now, cold it's been
though I cannot speak to you,
for you are lying as if on sand
while I, as in a pew.

And so, my friend
of years gone by,
if ever you choose to stand,
please let me know,
I ask you,
and I
will grasp your hand.

There are no words to express the abyss between isolation and
having one ally. It may be conceded to the mathematician that
four is twice two. But two is not twice one; two is two thousand
times one. G.K. Chesterton

People are meant to go through life two by two. 'T'ain't natural
to be lonesome.
Our Town, Thornton Wilder

Now friendship may be thus defined: a complete accord on all
subjects human and divine, joined with mutual good will and
affection. And with the exception of wisdom, I am inclined to
think nothing better than this has been given to man by the

immortal gods.
The real friend . . . is, as it were, another self. Cicero

Going Without Saying (In memory of Joe Flynn)
Bernard O'Donoghue

It is a great pity we don't know
When the dead are going to die.
So that, over a last companionable
Drink, we could tell them.

Happy the man who, dying, can
Place his hand on his heart and say:
'At least I didn't neglect to tell
The thrush how beautifully she sings.'

On Friendship

Your friend is your needs answered. He is your field which you
sow with love and reap with thanksgiving. And he is your board
and your fireside. For you come to him with your hunger, and
you seek him for peace. When your friend speaks his mind you
fear not the "nay" in your own mind, nor do you withhold the
"ay." And when he is silent your heart ceases not to listen to his
heart; For without words, in friendship, all thoughts, all desires,
all expectations are born and shared, with joy that is
unacclaimed. When you part from your friend, you grieve not;
For that which you love most in him may be clearer in his
absence, as the mountain to the climber is clearer from the plain.
And let there be no purpose in friendship save the deepening of
the spirit. For love that seeks aught but the disclosure of its own
mystery is not love but a net cast forth: and only the unprofitable
is caught. And let your best be for your friend. If he must know
the ebb of your tide, let him know its flood also. For what is your
friend that you should seek him with hours to kill? Seek him

always with hours to live. For it is his to fill your need, but not your emptiness. And in the sweetness of friendship let there be laughter, and sharing of pleasures. For in the dew of little things the heart finds its morning and is refreshed.

Gibran Khalil Gibran, The Prophet

Think where man's glory
most begins and ends,
and say my glory was
I had such friends
William Butler Yeats

When we honestly ask ourselves which person in our lives means the most to us, we often find that it is those who, instead of giving much advice, solutions, or cures, have chosen rather to share our pain and touch our wounds with a gentle and tender hand. The friend who can be silent with us in a moment of despair or confusion, who can stay with us in an hour of grief and bereavement, who can tolerate not knowing, not curing, not healing and face with us the reality of our powerlessness, that is a friend who cares.
- - - Henri Nouwen "Out of Solitude"

I know that people come to change... we'll grow apart. We'll pass, with age... And so our friendship is a phase. But how I've loved these days. Author unknown

---

"Ubuntu": South African saying means, "I am because we are."

T. S. Eliot, The Cocktail Party:

… we die to each other daily. What we know of other people is only our memory of the moments during which we knew them. And they have changed since then.

Epicurus tells us that "of all the things that wisdom provides to help one live one's entire life in happiness, the greatest by far is the possession of friendship."

"They're a two man party in a movable tavern where it's never closing time," says a woman of her husband and his lifelong buddy sitting offshore in a small rowboat, laughing and talking and semi-fishing.   Robert Fulghum's book "Words I Wish I Wrote."

"He would walk into my mind as if it were a town and he a torchlight procession of one, lighting up the streets..."

 Words of a graveside eulogy of one friend for another, as related by Nobel Prize-winning poet Seamus Heaney in his book The Redress of Poetry.

Do not believe that the person who is trying to offer you solace lives his life effortlessly among the simple and quiet words that might occasionally comfort you. His life is filled with much hardship and sadness, and it remains far behind yours. But if it were otherwise, he could never have found these words.
>   The Wisdom of Rilke

"I don't like that man. I must get to know him better." Abraham Lincoln

---

Friendship is a mirror to presence and a testament to forgiveness. Friendship not only helps us see ourselves through another's eyes, but can be sustained over the years only with someone who has repeatedly forgiven us for our trespasses as we must find it in ourselves to forgive them in turn. A friend knows our difficulties and shadows and remains in sight, a companion to our vulnerabilities more than our triumphs, when we are under the strange illusion wed do not need them. . . .

All friendships of any length are based on a continued, mutual forgiveness. Without tolerance and mercy all friendships die.

Consolations. The Solace, Nourishment and Underlying Meaning of Every Day Words David Whyte

---

In the course of the years a close friendship will always reveal the shadow in the other as much as ourselves, to remain friends we must know the other and their difficulties and even their sins and encourage the best in them, not through critique but through addressing the better part of them, the leading creative edge of their incarnation, thus subtly discouraging what makes them smaller, less generous, less of themselves.

Through the eyes of a real friendship an individual is larger than their everyday actions, and through the eyes of another we receive a greater sense of our own personhood, one we can aspire to, the one in whom they have most faith.

Consolations. The Solace, Nourishment and Underlying

Begin. Open. *Anywhere.*

Meaning of Every Day Words David Whyte

They told me, Heraclitus; they told me you were dead.

They brought me bitter news to hear, and bitter tears to shed.

I wept when I remembered how often you and I

Had tired the sun with talking, and sent him down the sky.

From William Cory's translation of the poem by
Callimachus about his beloved friend Heraclitus. (But Enough
About You, Christopher Buckley)

The most important things are the hardest to say. They are the
things you get ashamed of, because words diminish them —
words shrink things that seemed limitless when they were in your
head to no more than living size when they're brought out. But
it's more than that, isn't it? The most important things lie too
close to wherever your secret heart is buried, like landmarks to a
treasure your enemies would love to steal away. And you may
make revelations that cost you dearly only to have people look at
you in a funny way, not understanding what you've said at all, or
why you thought it was so important that you almost cried while
you were saying it. That's the worst, I think. When the secret
stays locked within not for want of a teller but for want of an
understanding ear. Stephen King, Different Seasons

"Alright then, I'll go to hell." – Mark Twain, The Adventures of Huckleberry Finn.

[Huck has been led to believe it would be sinful to help his friend Jim, a runaway slave. In this chapter, Huck finds his own moral compass and decides to do what he feels is the right thing, even though others have told him he would go to hell for it.]

"'Why did you do all this for me?' he asked. 'I don't deserve it. I've never done anything for you.' 'You have been my friend,' replied Charlotte. 'That in itself is a tremendous thing.'" E.B. White, Charlotte's Web

---

I don't want every one to like me; I should think less of myself if some people did.
-Henry James, The Portrait of a Lady

Gratitude

Sometimes all we need to do
is envision her wrapped in a ribbon—
to remind ourselves
of just how precious she is.

There isn't one word for it,
but there are many.

It's the wings helping us up,
as if they were a part of us
that belonged.

It's the tears of a loving friend
that join with ours
to make ours more bearable.

It's the life within us
when we survive,
and feel the hope of another day.

It's the kind word—
either for us, or from us.

It's every moment we dig down
to search for who we really are,
and find the goodness
we had forgotten.

It's every single struggle,
every pain,
every challenge,

that has changed us for the better.

It's all the weaknesses of yesterday
that no longer are,
and all the wisdom from that day
that's new.

It is every time we come to a fork in life
that would have us choose
between two paths built by others,
but choose instead
to forge a new path of our own.

It's that space between
the moment before and the moment after,
that squeezes from us the feeling
that we are doing right.

It's the something
that leans us forward
for that moment
only we can make happen.

It is the pauses that follow the glory
that add to the glory.

It is *Gratitude*—
for all that we have available to us
that simply cannot be captured
in one word.

The Good Teacher

They remember
the waters that slowed them,
the hills that tired them,
and the skies that frightened them.

They remember it all—
Everything they had to push through
to make it.
They knew your journey best,
because they remembered theirs.

Their language was your language—
the same language they needed
when *they* were young.

They understood
how it was
that you couldn't understand,
because they remembered
that one day, long ago,
they couldn't understand either.

They struggled too.

They are *the Good Teacher.*

So, if you're ever wondering
why it is
that you have struggled
so much in your life
—why you have sometimes been

slowed, and tired, and frightened—
keep your eyes out
for others who need help—

They are the reason.

"I had a good day today. Thank you."

(A simple prayer of gratitude that always makes a good day
better.)

This morning two friends and I talked of our sons.
My friends are younger.
One of their sons is in high school, the other in grade school.
Mine are long past school.

But it made no difference—they are *parents*,
just as I am a parent,
and they talked of the love of *love*,
how children take our lives
and transform them,
how good gratitude feels,
and how accomplished children are
at helping us feel it.

I felt it. This morning. Just listening.

They talked of time . . . spending time
with their sons—how important it is,
and how special.

They talked of urgency, how
it won't be long
before their sons are grown,
before their sons leave home,
fall in love,
have children
of their own.

They know that.

I listened,
and was thankful
for the window of my office
that pointed to the basketball hoop in our driveway,
and for all the times I left work
to rebound for my sons.
It wasn't just about rebounding.

Neither of my friends have the window I had,
but you wouldn't know it.

They're lucky—
They see today
how lucky today is.

Gratitude helps us relive the joys that it celebrates. I recently
thought of a past Thanksgiving Day for which I am most grateful
to my loving wife, to whom I have dedicated this book. I include
it in this chapter on Gratitude as a small example of the benefits
of Gratitude—When we feel thankful, we feel better.

Diane had prepared a wonderful Thanksgiving dinner and I
couldn't eat any of it. She had worked on the dinner from the day

before Thanksgiving, chopping vegetables for home-made stuffing and peeling and mashing sweet potatoes.

Unfortunately, I came down with symptoms of exhaustion, chills, dizziness, sweats, headaches, eye aches, nausea and very-painful-to-the-touch face, neck and scalp. I couldn't get out of bed. It was bad. Diane ate Thanksgiving dinner alone. I had no appetite.

Right from the start, though, she did absolutely everything she could to take care of me: She encouraged me to drink water throughout the day, bringing me bedside bottle after bottle. She tried to get me to eat so that I would have strength. (I didn't eat anything until 6:00 PM when she brought me home-made chicken noodle soup and Ritz crackers saying, "You have to have something to eat!" She had offered to cook me anything.) She massaged my head. She sponge-bathed my face and body, and shampooed my hair. She took phenomenal care of me.

This morning she offered to make me anything I wanted for breakfast (to get me to eat). I chose oatmeal, mixed berries and maple syrup. And she just now reminded me again to "drink water." For lunch, she again tried to get me to eat by cutting up the turkey into bite-sized pieces, and brought me watermelon too. I'm still not back to normal, but I'm much better than I would be without Diane.

This Thanksgiving Day—*Diane*, really—reminded me that we can be both broken and blessed. As much as it feels good to be lucky, it feels even better to be thankful. I am very lucky, and thankful, to have Diane as my wife.

When we have spent most of our adult lives working, hopefully

we have spent them working at a job that has rewarded us and

are thankful for those rewards. I spent my career as a trial lawyer. Here is an essay of gratitude for those years as a trial lawyer.

A Lawyer's Gratitude: 5 Reasons to Become a Trial Lawyer—All Between the Verdicts

Gareth H. Caldbeck, Esq.

When you've spent most of your adult life as a trial lawyer you enjoy experiences—including relationships—that you don't reflect on at the time ... because you're too busy being a trial lawyer. I have had a chance now to reflect on my experiences, my colleagues and my adversaries, and I'm grateful for them. Verdicts are what you live on, but memories are what you live for.

I want to share with you five reasons to become a trial lawyer, all of which have left me with memories that add to my life. I want to share them with those of you who are still at it, because I know that sometimes we don't appreciate what we have. Although my experiences stem from my life as a trial lawyer, I'm sure they resemble what takes place daily in your life—whether or not you are a trial lawyer. Whatever the nature of your law practice, I hope that my own reflections will help you appreciate your own experiences.

There are more than five, of course, but trial lawyers are busy—even those who are just thinking of becoming a trial lawyer are busy—so I've limited this list to five. Five are enough to get you started on your own. Here they are.

1. Clients

They become a purpose in your life. Not every one, of course. But every once in a while—you never know when—someone will sit across from you in your office and tell you his[1] story. And it will be a story that needs you, and one that you need, really—to be able someday to feel that you made a difference.

Not every job puts you in a position to be trusted with someone's life story (a story that can substantially change his life). The job of a trial lawyer does. Not every job enables you to make a person's life better, to make him whole again, to

---

[1] I've chosen to use the male reference only to avoid the cumbersome he/she, etc. Everything I say applies as well to "her."

compensate him for what life has taken away. The job of a trial lawyer does. And not every job can leave you with a feeling that—at least for some—you made a good difference in their lives. The job of a trial lawyer does that too. As a trial lawyer, you get to help people.

That's only a part of it, though. Think of the opportunities your clients have given *you*:

You've witnessed a young mother remain steadfast in her belief that her brain-damaged daughter will recover; you've seen her massage every stiffened limb of her child over and over and over again, talk for hours to her child's glazed eyes and see sparkles no one else could, and laugh at times when reason for grief so filled the room that laughter itself was a miracle.

You've grown to know the young man charged with multiple counts of burglary—born in a family in which every one of his brothers was in jail—who had lied about his age to join the Marines when he was fifteen. He wanted, you come to understand, to get away from the legacy his family offered him, and you not only believe him, you believe *in* him, as did the judge.

You've been paid back a thousand-fold by an old serial criminal client—one you had represented many years earlier (for possession of stolen property)—when you called to ask him to keep an eye out for your great-grandfather's gold pocket-watch that had been stolen from you. "I just bought it for $100, Gareth," he said. "It's yours. I owe you."

You've heard the wail of your client, the good man who contracted Legionnaire's Disease, as he reacted in the courtroom to his doctor's powerful testimony that he would die from it.

You have cried with and for parents who have lost their son, and felt the enormity of a parent's love.

You have seen more suffering and more strength than you thought possible. You have had good clients ... and you have learned and grown from their losses and their strengths.

2. Colleagues/Adversaries

We may not see them every day, or even talk to them every day, but every day they enter our minds. The same lawyers who keep us up at night, the ones who know our case as well as we do, the ones who will be prepared at trial, the ones who have beaten us in the past, or might have—these are the lawyers who have made us work even harder. They are the ones who have forced us to hone our skills, if not to be better, at least to compete. They are the ones who have molded us into the trial attorneys we have become. They are (I can say this now) our role models. If and when their respect comes to us, we can believe it has been earned. Their respect is an honor.

I consider myself lucky to have worked with and against lawyers from whom I could learn. They made me a much better lawyer.

Think of them. Surely, they are in your life as well:

The Machine, for example—the one who seemingly does it all without effort, and quickly. His organization is unparalleled. His speech is quick, his mind quicker. He not only knows the law, he knows chapter and verse exactly which opinions govern the facts of your case (which, unfortunately for you, is also his).

Then there's the Eloquent One. You wish you had the luxury of drifting off to his words, basking in them as you would the sun, but you don't. He's arguing (and so artfully) against you. Why, you wonder, aren't there such wonderful words to describe your side of the case. But you know that there are. You even know some of them. It's not only a matter of vocabulary, you realize; it's a matter of his putting them together in ways that you can't. You console yourself by thinking that he doesn't bring the same passion to the case that you do, and then you notice them— the tears, welling in his eyes.

And the Respected One. He is the one who must have earned his right to make mistakes, because not only are they overlooked, they bring us—the judge as well—only to believe that he will correct them on his own, and in due time. It may all simply be a ploy.

And the Fair One. He is the one we all admire and like. How, we wonder, can he have the excellent reputation he enjoys, *as a trial lawyer* after all, and yet be so <u>fair</u>? He's the one chosen to sit as an arbitrator between you and the other biased person on the arbitration panel. He apparently has mastered the ability to see both sides of a story, reminding you that you still have work to do as a trial lawyer.

And the Clever One. The others may bother you, but this guy gets under your skin. Did he really have to hire your expert's <u>mentor</u> as his expert?

And the Smooth One. It may be small, but it's noticeable. There is a difference between the Eloquent One and the Smooth One. The Smooth One—if he is to be thought of as the Smooth One—needs to be *too* smooth. Slippery, that's the word. We don't mind this one … because jurors do. "Go on," we whisper under our breath, "you're on a roll." His problem is that no one cares which way he rolls, with the probable exception of himself.

We know them all, as colleagues and adversaries. And from them—from each of them—we learn. That alone warrants the gratitude I feel for having known them. In the end, the better your colleagues and the better your adversaries the more you learn. You work with and against highly skilled advocates and negotiators. You learn from them.

3. Experts

"I can't guarantee that he had an aneurysm," the Harvard neuropathologist told me, "but I can guarantee that if he had one I will find it." These are the words of an expert. Experts are those to whom we throw pieces of the puzzle with the hope that they will put them neatly together. The trial lawyer must first envision the puzzle's solution, but, in fairness, it is the expert upon whom we rely to make certain that the pieces fit.

Even more— they make *us* experts. Sometimes it's our own experts who teach us, but most often it's the opponents' experts who force us to learn. And we do. And learning—the learning of so much in so many diverse areas—is one great reason to become a trial lawyer.

This is your story if you are a trial lawyer. You have taken a case involving a defective product, a baby's rattle, for example. You have no idea how rattles are designed, or why they're designed as they are. You do know, though, that your clients' daughter choked on one. You know that she suffered irreparable and profound brain damage because that rattle was small enough to fit down her tiny throat, yet large enough to get stuck in it. You know that's wrong; it shouldn't happen. And so you start the trial lawyer's journey: you research the law; you research the facts; you meet with experts in baby rattle design; you discover similar experiences with similar products, or even the same product. And you meet again with other experts. And you listen, and learn.

And you learn things that the rattle manufacturer should have learned long ago—far before this little girl's life was irreparably altered: toddlers put rattles in their mouths. Toddlers are learning to walk. Most likely, toddlers will walk with their rattle in their mouth. They will fall. They will fall with the rattle in their mouth. That rattle, if small enough, will be forced into that child's throat. The worst possible size for a rattle is one small enough to slip down a throat, yet large enough to be difficult to extract. You learn of previous complaints, concerns, accidents, injuries, even deaths.

And then you learn the medical side of your case. You

learn how profound brain damage affects not only the victim's ability to think and speak; it affects her entire body, contracting her limbs in ways that make manifest the severity of damage to her brain. It even affects her life expectancy. How much it does is another contested issue. Does she need medical bills paid, for example, another ten years, or fifty years? You need to learn about this too.

Early and steadfast denials of liability have turned to admission and settlement. And as a trial lawyer you have again been blessed to have stood behind the resolve of young, determined, and loving parents. And you have—as with all other cases—learned life lessons. The effect of just one of these lessons is that you will watch more closely the toys of the toddlers in your own life.

In the end, you realize that you have learned not only from *your* experts in the case, but *because* of your adversary's experts. You don't let them claim that your profoundly brain-damaged child will die within five years, for example. You search out every reputable article you can find that contradicts or weakens their argument. You contact the authors of the articles. They become your experts.

Sometimes it's you who has to bring the evidence to your expert. And you do. As for experts that your adversaries call to testify, you come to understand that although a given expert has spent a lifetime in a field, he has not spent a lifetime answering the questions you have prepared for his cross-examination. And it should show. You know as much as he does in this area, or, if not, you know enough to make it appear that you do. Which means, of course, that you will have learned even more about life.

4. Judges

The best judges in my life were also my mentors—lawyers who had stood as trial lawyers in the same courtrooms as I, who believed in me, who knew what changes I needed to make if I were to move to the next level, and who took the time to critique me, to give me tips, to help me learn. This is the mindset that makes the difference. Most judges can find and apply the law, or have law clerks who can, but the judge who does more than write opinions is the judge who not only does his best to render justice; he changes young lawyers' lives.

Of course it's not the job of a judge to mentor attorneys. I see that. But those who do, those who care enough to provide not only constructive feedback, but encouragement, work their influence long before—and long after—they have made their decisions and written their opinions. I am grateful to have had several judges in my career who took the time to talk with me after trials, provided either positive feedback that encouraged me to continue, or gave me helpful critiques that made me a more effective advocate.

I'm thankful to the judge, for example, who suggested to me that I argue only three points in my closing arguments. More than this, he said, the jury can't follow or remember. He wouldn't worry if at times I felt compelled to argue four points. At least I had learned that I shouldn't argue four until I had done my very best to limit myself to three.

I'm thankful to the judge who suggested to me that I

slow down on cross-examination. Allow the jury time to savor the fruit you've picked. Cross-examination is your time to testify. You are the one testifying; you're the one speaking to the jury. Don't tell your story so quickly that they can't absorb it.

I'm thankful to the justice, for whom I clerked, for laboring over his opinions—the writing of which did not come easily to him—until they said exactly what he wanted. For the justice who criticized him for the number of drafts it might have taken him, the poet William Butler Yeats had the answer: *"Those friends of mine/ Who do me wrong/ Whenever I remake a song/ Should know what issue is at stake /It is myself that I remake."*[2]

My justice set high goals for himself in the drafting of his opinions. It wasn't easy for him to reach those goals. But he kept at it. So what if it irritated another justice; he was remaking himself. It's a good lesson for all of us when we're struggling in life, and are criticized. You believe in yourself—you believe in your cause. You are a trial lawyer.

I am thankful to the judge who allowed me to treat my

---

[2] William Butler Yeats, preliminary poem, *in* 2 The Collected Works in Verse and Prose of William Butler Yeats (1908).

own expert as a hostile witness (to allow for leading questions) because the expert had developed Alzheimer's Disease shortly before trial but had submitted a twenty-page disclosure letter to the defendants when he was of sounder mind.

I'm thankful to every judge who took his time to help me, to the judges who listened to me and showed me respect, to those who showed my clients respect. Any judge can judge. All of us, in fact, do it too freely. Those who make a difference—those I am thankful to have worked with—are the ones who make every effort to make the process a fair one. They listen to you. They let you know that they understand your position. They are patient. They show you respect. They help you on your path to becoming a better attorney. They remember how difficult it is to walk the tightrope of a courtroom.

Ironically, the donning of a judge's robe uncovers the character of the person who wears it. Whether or not his experience on the way to judgeship has enlightened him is far less important than where and how and why he shines what light he has.

5. Fear and Uncertainty

You have done your best. Your client, the Pope, could not have been more persuasive. It's almost as if the cardinals' testimony was overkill. Yet there you stand, watching for favorable eye contact with just one of the jurors (even if only the one wearing the habit) as they march into the courtroom to deliver the verdict … and you are trembling.

I'm not thankful for the times I trembled, but I am thankful for the times I could resist the shaking of my body, forcing myself to keep in mind that I had met my obligations. I had done my best; the rest was out of my control—a lesson from the serenity prayer … and from the courtroom.

A trial lawyer who is unafraid is most likely a trial lawyer who is unprepared. I never tried a case when I wasn't afraid. You need to remember: when you start to sweat, when your body shakes, when your heart pounds, when every part of you wishes you were somewhere else, look out—courage has a chance to be born.

I was afraid that my discovery might be inadequate. I was afraid that a deposition might give away more than I got. I was afraid when I met with insurance adjusters and/or opposing attorneys that I would appear unprepared or unconfident. I was afraid of the law, that I might have missed a critical statute or case. I was afraid of voir dire—not only that I might fail to ask the right questions, but that I would have no idea how to interpret the answers to the questions I did ask. I was afraid of my opening statement, that I might overstate my case, forget to say all that I had intended to say or, worst of all, not convey powerfully that I believed in my client. I was afraid that my direct examinations would leave it for the jury to seek out what I had assumed would be obvious to them. I was afraid that my cross-examinations would be more fire than light, making the witness more likable, and myself less. I was afraid that my closing arguments—my final opportunity to persuade—would not reflect that I was a lawyer to be respected and trusted, that I believed in the justice of my client's cause, that there were good reasons for my belief, and that those reasons merited the passion in my argument. I was afraid the jurors might not feel as strongly as I did.

Fear can cripple, and I acknowledge that it stopped me from doing things I wish I had, but in the end its name is on every favorable verdict I earned, and it was with me—so often—to encourage me to prepare more. The fearful may suffer, but the overconfident fail. I am thankful for all that my fears forced me to do, and my fear-driven success as a trial lawyer serves as a reminder today, in life, that the best goals are most often the most difficult, and what's most difficult is usually most feared. Appreciate your fear in the courtroom and in life. It may well mean that you've set your goals high, and that you're on the right path to reaching them.

Happiness

Happiness is always to be found where you need to be looking—
outward.

What might have been, is true for everyone. *What is,* is true only for you.

Your time is better spent on *what is.*

There will always be the bend in the road ahead
that beckons.
But let it wait—
Explore, search,
find and feel
what is here
and now.

Happiness is a state, and it has nothing to do with where you are.
It's where you think you are. If you don't like where you think
you are, think to a different state.

We were never meant to be happy for ourselves.
We were meant to be happy with ourselves
for the good we do for others.

Resolutions

I want to attend to those things in my life
I can change for the better.

Those things I can't change, I want to learn to accept.

Above all—having these two simple resolutions in mind—
I want to appreciate the power of *Now.*

If one only wished to be happy, this could be easily
accomplished; but we wish to be happier than other people, and
this is always difficult, for we believe others to be happier than
they are. Montesquieu

There ought to be behind the door of every happy, contented man
someone standing with a hammer, continually reminding him
with a tap that there are unhappy people. Anton Chekov

For as this appalling ocean surrounds the verdant land, so in the
soul of man there lies one insular Tahiti, full of peace and joy,
but encompassed by all the horrors of the half-lived life.

Herman Melville, Moby Dick

Happiness is like a butterfly; the more you chase it, the more it
will elude you, but if you turn your attention to other things, it
will come and sit softly on your shoulder. Thoreau

Consider the person who lets frivolities dominate him
completely, until he becomes quite beside himself with all his

pointless amusements and stupid crazes; such an individual may believe himself to be living happily, but the more he is convinced that this is so, the more desperately miserable his existence really is. Cicero

---

All who joy would win
Must share it,
Happiness was born a twin   Lord Byron

Nine Promises that can bring Happiness

Promise yourself that you will talk health, happiness, and prosperity as often as possible.
Promise yourself to make all your friends know there is something in them that is special and that you value.
Promise to think only of the best, to work only for the best, and to expect only the best in yourself and others.
Promise to be just as enthusiastic about the success of others as you are about your own.

Promise yourself to be so strong that nothing can disturb your peace of mind.
Promise to forget the mistakes of the past and press on to greater achievements in the future.
Promise to wear a cheerful appearance at all times and give every person you meet a smile.
Promise to give so much time to improving yourself that you have no time to criticize others.

Promise to be too large for worry, too noble for anger, too strong for fear, and too happy to permit trouble to press on you.

John Wooden, Wooden

She unfolded the money, then pushed it up her sleeve, "Whatchyouwant?" she asked Richard, suspiciously. "Nothing," said Richard. "I really don't want anything. Nothing at all." And then he realized how true that was; and how dreadful a thing it had become. "Have you ever got everything you ever wanted and then realized it wasn't what you wanted at all?"

Neverwhere. Neil Gaiman.

To laugh often and much; to win the respect of intelligent people and affection of children; to earn the appreciation of honest critics and endure the betrayal of false friends; to appreciate beauty, to find the best in others; to leave the world a bit better, whether by a healthy child, a garden patch or a redeemed social condition; to know even one life has breathed easier because you have lived. This is to have succeeded.
Ralph Waldo Emerson

In "Going to Walden," the poet Mary Oliver reflects on the complex "message" of Thoreau. In her poem, she responds to friends who suggest that she drive to Walden Pond for a day trip, to get in touch with the meaning of Thoreau's masterwork. She resists going on this physical journey, suggesting that

> Going to Walden is not so easy a thing
> As a green visit. It is the slow and difficult
> Trick of living, and finding it where you are.

Promised Land, Thirteen Books that Changed America, Jay Parini

Humor

If you're going through a difficult time in your life and someone says, "You'll laugh about this in 30 years," it's not the 30 years that will work the magic; it's the laughter.

Friends enter our lives one laugh at a time.

Our last goodbye
was everything I thought it would be.
and more.
I cried when we had to pull apart,
thinking of how much I really loved her,
her laugh, her smile,
all that we had shared.

And when she finally turned to walk away,
slowly,
so "*she-must-know-I-am-looking*" slowly,
I just couldn't stop
staring
and thinking . . .
I really will miss her.

Playing Poker

I love a good game of cards, poker.
I love how he thinks he understands the others,
that somehow he's the best,
how he wants to believe he plays the worst of hands
better than others play more gifted cards
and does ...
believe, that is.

I love how we dress up good luck
in a suit of skill
as if to fool ourselves
into believing that the suit is a part of us,
or how a mistimed bluff
(any bluff before a call)
was clever
(and should have been respected,)

or the leaning on tomorrow –
always the "next time" –
and the promise we find in our future
for a better showing,
our thinking that inevitability is on our side
and that our jack-high lives
and six-high skill
will always turn to aces
at the table.

[A Christmas Greeting I sent out to friends and family when I had neglected to create or buy normal Christmas cards.]

Greetings, Family and Friends!

I need your help, and trust that Christmas would be a good time to ask for it—which brings me to Christmas, actually, and the fact that you have not received the picture-card from us that I unfortunately had promised Diane I would prepare and order some time ago.

The favor I need is this:

Picture in your mind a photograph of Diane and me. It should be a good one. Imagine that it's on the cover of a beautiful, and, yes, expensive Christmas card (although trust me, this is not about money). The card may have its own nice message; it will likely have colors of red and green somewhere; it will be as large as you imagine it to be. It will make you smile and leave you with a good feeling about us, and yourself—really about our treasured friendship. I leave it all up to your preferences and imagination.

Imagine also that we have written a message personal to you. Handwritten. One that recalls a special time in our lives when each of us felt the glow of our bond brightening. For this, I ask not that you use your imagination, but your memory. Indulge yourself in the best of our times.

Recall the smiles, the laughter. Recall that you were with us also during the sad times, and we were with you. Do this after you have closed the card that you have created. As you close your eyes, reflect, if only for a moment, on the fact that although I have failed in getting to you the card I had wanted, you are special in our lives, and, because of that, I have asked this favor of you.

I know that your card will be exactly as I had hoped.

Thank you for helping me. Diane and I are thankful to have you in our lives, and wish you a very Merry Christmas and a wonderful New Year!

Love, Gareth and Diane

Humor is common sense, dancing. William James

"All right, they are on our left. They're on our right. They're in front of us. They're behind us - they can't get away from us this time!" U.S. Marine Chesty Puller surrounded by enemy forces during Korean War

The Difference Maker by John C. Maxwell

Franklin Pierce Adams, a journalist, belonged to a poker group that included an actor named Herbert Ransom. Whenever Ransom held a good hand, his facial expression was so transparent that Adams proposed a new rule for the club: "Anyone who looks at Ransom's face is cheating."

When choosing between two evils, I always like to try the one I've never tried before.
Mae West

There are three types of people in this world: those who make things happen, those who watch things happen, and those who wonder what happened. Mary Kay Ash

---

Just before takeoff on an airplane flight, the stewardess reminded Mohammed Ali to fasten his seatbelt. "Superman don't need no seatbelt", replied Ali. "Superman don't need no airplane either", said the stewardess.

He has all the virtues I dislike and none of the vices I admire.
Winston Churchill

Scene from The Odd Couple, by Neil Simon
(two roommates having a discussion)
FELIX: (Sits at the table with a great pretense of calm): All right, Oscar, I'd like to know what's happened?
OSCAR: (Moves toward him): What's happened?
FELIX: (Hurriedly slides over to the next chair): That's right. Something must have caused you to go off the deep end like this. What is it? Something I said? Something I did? Heh? What?
OSCAR: (Pacing) It's nothing you said. It's nothing you did.

It's you!
FELIX: I see. Well, that's plain enough.
OSCAR: I could make it plainer but I don't want to hurt you.
FELIX: What is it, the cooking? The cleaning? The crying?
OSCAR: (Moving toward him): I'll tell you exactly what it is.
It's the cooking, cleaning and crying. It's the talking in your
sleep, it's the moose calls that open your ears at two o'clock in
the morning. I can't take it any more, Felix. I'm crackin' up.
Everything you do irritates me. And when you're not here, the
things I know you're gonna do when you come in irritate me.
You leave me little notes on my pillow. I told you a hundred
times, I can't stand little notes on my pillow. "We're all out of
Corn Flakes. F.U." It took me three hours to figure out that F.U.
was Felix Ungar. It's not your fault, Felix. It's a rotten
combination.
FELIX: I get the picture.
OSCAR: That's just the frame. The picture I haven't even
painted yet.

There was a neat true story in Bill Bryson's book (which deals
with Australia) about a 4-year-old little girl who befriended
construction workers building a home next to hers. She spent her
time with the construction workers, who "adopted" her as a
mascot, let her help out a little and actually paid her "half a
crown" at the end of the week. Her proud mother took her to the
bank to open an account. The banker asked the little 4-year-old
how she had earned her money. She replied, "by helping build a
house." The banker then asked her if she would be building a
house next week. "We will", the little girl said, "if we ever get
the fucking bricks."

In A Sunburned Country, by Bill Bryson

The only problem with Haiku is that you just get started and then
~ Roger McGough

A man who ignored a line of people at a ticket counter in an airport, went up and said, "You have to get me on this plane, and I need a first class seat." "Sorry," said the ticket agent, "I'm helping these people now. When I can I will help you." The man yelled back, angrily, "Do you know who I am?". Immediately, without missing a beat, she reached under the counter and pulled up the phone to make an announcement over the intercom system. "Attention, everyone. May I please have your attention. There is a man at the American Airlines ticket counter who apparently does not know who he is."

The Porcupine's Kisses by Stephen Dobyns, a great book of poetry, unusual in that it contains many one liners, and definitions. For example:

well-meaning: offers to teach your wife a trick or two

Wiles: the fox rents a wheelchair

Winner: future loser

Wish: when now isn't enough

Yesterday: the almost preceding today's not quite

Zero: waits while all the rest is lost

Unavailing: the chicken offers the fox an egg

Uncertain: pretty girl, old condom

Ubiquitous: the temptations you can barely resist

Uglier: the children of your friends

Ugliness: anything looked at too briefly or too long

Tranquility: ask the cow

Topless: the sudden revelation of opportunities lost

Thrifty: drops a smile in the beggar's cup

soon: the last guarantee to lose its luster

A sampling of one liners:

The world seeks to erase itself; you work to make its details survive. What you love are such details.

Part of him felt more comfortable in the dark. The part that insisted on turning on the light.

The seamless arguments he wove by day, the night found the flaws.

The mansion of his ambition - he was a fly buzzing against its basement windows.

When I ask you for something, I ask you for everything.

Ashamed to ask why, he learned to say because.

He tried to make his children his second chance and they too turned out badly.

When he argues, other people's ideas show through the holes of his own.

He felt his judgments enlarged him; he grew larger when he refused to judge.

It's not events that make him afraid; his imagination makes him afraid.

Once again spring approaches. Birds begin their eager songs. Feel glad you can still be over-swept.

Looking at someone else, the first thing I look for is something of myself.

Mistakes aren't the enemy; regret is the enemy.

Every bad idea has a good reason.

When he counts his blessings he counts the evils that have happened to you.

By envying another's success I become part of that success.

The moments he remembers - they would fill a single day.

After they gave him the prize, he dedicated his life to building his statue.

Young, he thought the answers lay ahead; older now, he thinks they must lie behind.

You are the song you are learning to sing.

> The Porcupine's Kisses by Stephen Dobyns

[The Mississippi Legislature had been debating Prohibition when Noah S. "Soggy" Sweat (a state congressman and later a circuit court judge and college professor) gave this speech.]

My friends, I had not intended to discuss this controversial subject at this particular time. However, I want you to know that I do not shun controversy. On the contrary, I will take a stand on any issue at any time, regardless of how fraught with controversy it might be. You have asked me how I feel about whiskey. All right, here is how I feel about whiskey.

If you mean whiskey, the devil's brew, the poison scourge, the bloody monster that defiles innocence, dethrones reason, destroys the home, creates misery and poverty, yea, literally takes the bread from the mouths of little children; if you mean that evil drink that topples Christian men and women from the pinnacles of righteous and gracious living into the bottomless pits of degradation, shame, despair, helplessness, and hopelessness, then, my friend, I am opposed to it with every fiber of my being.

However, if by whiskey you mean the oil of conversation, the philosophic wine, the elixir of life, the ale that is consumed when good fellows get together, that puts a song in their hearts and the warm glow of contentment in their eyes; if you mean Christmas cheer, the stimulating sip that puts a little spring in the step of an elderly gentleman on a frosty morning; if you mean that drink that enables man to magnify his joy, and to forget life's great tragedies and heartbreaks and sorrow; if you mean that drink the sale of which pours into our treasuries untold millions of dollars each year, that provides tender care for our little crippled children, our blind, our deaf, our dumb, our pitifully aged and infirm, to build the finest highways, hospitals, universities, and community colleges in this nation, then my friend, I am absolutely, unequivocally in favor of it.

This is my position, and as always, I refuse to be compromised on matters of principle.

By the time you swear you're his,
Shivering and sighing,
And he vows his passion is
Infinite, undying –
Lady, make note of this:
One of you is lying.

Dorothy Parker, "Unfortunate Coincidence"

---

may i feel said he
by: e.e. cummings

may i feel said he
(i'll squeal said she
just once said he)
it's fun said she

(may i touch said he
how much said she
a lot said he)
why not said she

(let's go said he
not too far said she
what's too far said he
where you are said she)

may i stay said he
(which way said she
like this said he
if you kiss said she

may i move said he
is it love said she)
if you're willing said he
(but you're killing said she

but it's life said he
but your wife said she
now said he)
ow said she

(tiptop said he
don't stop said she
oh no said he)
go slow said she

(cccome? said he
ummm said she)
you're divine! said he
(you are Mine said she)

Scintillate, Roger McGough

I have outlived
my youthfulness
so a quiet life for me

Where once
I use to
scintillate

now I sin
till ten
past three.

Deep Thoughts, by Jack Handey

It takes a big man to cry, but it takes a bigger man to laugh at that man.

One thing kids like is to be tricked. For instance, I was going to take my little nephew to Disneyland, but instead I drove him to an old burned-out warehouse. "Oh, no," I said. "Disneyland burned down." He cried and cried, but I think that deep down, he thought it was a pretty good joke. I started to drive over to the real Disneyland, but it was getting pretty late.

Dad always thought laughter was the best medicine, which I guess is why several of us died of tuberculosis.

Maybe in order to understand mankind, we have to look at the word itself: "Mankind". Basically, it's made up of two separate words - "mank" and "ind". What do these words mean ? It's a mystery, and that's why so is mankind.

When you go in for a job interview, I think a good thing to ask is if they ever press charges.

To me, clowns aren't funny. In fact, they're kind of scary. I've wondered where this started and I think it goes back to the time I went to the circus, and a clown killed my dad.

The memories of my family outings are still a source of strength to me. I remember we'd all pile into the car - I forget what kind it was - and drive and drive. I'm not sure where we'd go, but I think there were some trees there. The smell of something was strong in the air as we played whatever sport we played. I remember a bigger, older guy we called "Dad." We'd eat some stuff, or not, and then I think we went home. I guess some things never leave you.

If a kid asks where rain comes from, I think a cute thing to tell him is "God is crying." And if he asks why God is crying, another cute thing to tell him is "Probably because of something you did."

We used to laugh at Grandpa when he'd head off and go fishing. But we wouldn't be laughing that evening when he'd come back with some whore he picked up in town.

The crows seemed to be calling his name, thought Caw.

I can't stand cheap people. It makes me real mad when someone says something like, "Hey, when are you going to pay me that $100 you owe me?" or "Do you have that $50 you borrowed?" Man, quit being so cheap!

I wish I lived back in the old west days, because I'd save up my money for about twenty years so I could buy a solid-gold pick. Then I'd go out West and start digging for gold. When someone came up and asked what I was doing, I'd say, "Looking for gold, ya durn fool." He'd say, "Your pick is gold," and I'd say, "Well, that was easy." Good joke, huh.

A funny thing to do is, if you're out hiking and your friend gets bitten by a poisonous snake, tell him you're going to go for help, then go about ten feet and pretend that *you* got bit by a snake. Then start an argument with him about who's going to go get help. A lot of guys will start crying. That's why it makes you feel good when you tell them it was just a joke.

I remember that one fateful day when Coach took me aside. I knew what was coming. "You don't have to tell me," I said. "I'm off the team, aren't I?" "Well," said Coach, "you never were really ON the team. You made that uniform you're wearing out of rags and towels, and your helmet is a toy space helmet. You show up at practice and then either steal the ball and make us chase you to get it back, or you try to tackle people at inappropriate times." It was all true what he was saying. And yet, I thought something is brewing inside the head of this Coach. He sees something in me, some kind of raw talent that he can mold. But that's when I felt the handcuffs go on.

When I die, I would like to go peacefully, in my sleep, like my Grandfather did. Not screaming and yelling like the passenger in his car.

George Bernard Shaw was opening a play in London. He wrote a letter to Winston Churchill enclosing two box seat tickets to the opening night's performance. The letter said, "Enclosed are…. Please come, and bring a friend – if you have one." Churchill replied with a letter of his own. "Thank you for the tickets. Please send me two more, some seats for the next performance – if there is one."

"Oh come, now, you don't mean to let on that you like it?"
The brush continued to move.
"Like it? Well I don't see why I oughtn't to like it. Does a boy get a chance to whitewash a fence every day?"

That put the thing in a new light. Ben stopped nibbling his apple. Tom swept his brush daintily back and forthstepped back to note the effect – added a touch here and there – criticized the effect again – Ben watching every move and getting more and more interested, more and more absorbed.

Presently he said: "Say, Tom, let me whitewash a little."

 Mark Twain, The Adventures of Tom Sawyer

154

The poor guy was one dead dog from becoming a Country and Western song. Bobby Knight

---

Story told by General George Patton (from Killing Patton):

One of the bravest men I ever saw was on top of a telegraph pole in the midst of a furious fight in Tunisia. I stopped and asked what the hell he was doing up there at a time like that. He answered, "fixing the wire, sir". I asked, isn't that a little bit unhealthy right about now. He answered, Yes, sir, but the Goddamned wire has be fixed, sir. Don't the planes strafing the road bother you, I asked him. He answered, "No, sir, but you sure as hell do!"

I've been through lots of terrible things in my life. Some of them happened. Mark Twain

---

Why Old Men don't get hired:

Interviewer: Tell me your greatest weakness.
Old Man: Honesty
Interviewer: I don't think of honesty as a weakness.
Old Man: I don't give a Fuck what you think.

Man prays for a parking space, "God if you find me a parking space, I'll go to church every Sunday for the rest of my life." All of a sudden an empty parking space shows up. "Never mind, God," he says, "I found my own!" Lou Holtz, Franciscan University commencement speech.

Imagination

When I was a little boy I was both Superman and Davy Crockett. I never held a gun when I was Superman, and I never flew when I was Davy Crockett. Still, my Superman flew faster than "faster than a speeding bullet"; he not only leaped over tall buildings, he flew at the speed of light, and he was more powerful than thousands of "locomotives". He was everything.

And when I was Davy Crockett, no one was a better shooter, no one (except, on occasion, Jim Bowie) was better with a knife, and whether or not the real Davy Crockett carried a derringer hidden in his sock I don't know, but mine did. He was everything too, just like Superman.

At some point I stopped being Superman and Davy Crockett, but each of them taught me how to think, how to dream, how to imagine greatness in my life, and I am thankful to both of them for helping my imagination stay close enough to my talents to make at least a little sense, yet far enough away from them to stretch those talents. That's what imagination is for.

How great it is
that we don't count petals.
We just love them.

Thank you, Muhammad Ali, for helping us create in our own minds—as children and adults alike—our own arenas, at least once—filled with roaring fans. Thank you for having helped us dance around and pummel our own imagined opponents as if we were you, and thank you for helping us believe—if only for those moments—that we too were The Greatest.

So near I am to the little twig's end,
I think I feel the little twig bend.

Someday, I think, the twig may break
And I may fall and die.

I need to think instead, of course,
                                          fly.
                         to
                 learn
           to
     how
of

He's a man way out there in the blue, riding on a smile and a
shoeshine . . . A salesman is got to dream, boy.
Willy Loman's eulogy, The Death of a Salesman, Arthur Miller

There is a law in psychology that if you form a picture in your
mind of what you would like to be, and you keep and hold that
picture there long enough, you will soon become exactly as you
have been thinking.
William James, Psychologist and Author

If you were to assign letters of the alphabet to combinations of
digits, and were to do this for all human alphabets…then you
could fit any written character in any language to a combination
of digits in pi. According to this system, pi could be turned into
literature. Then, if you could look far enough into pi, you would
probably find the expression, "See the U.S.A in a Chevrolet!" a
billion times in a row. Elsewhere, you would find Christ's'
Sermon on the Mount in His native Aramaic tongue…. Also, you

would find a dictionary of Yanomamo curses. A guide to the pawnshops of Lubbock. The book about the sea which James Joyce supposedly declared he would write after he finished Finnegan's Wake. The collected transcripts of "The Tonight Show" rendered into Etruscan....

From The Elements of Story, by Francis Flaherty, quoting an article in The New Yorker by Richard Preston in an effort to convey the idea of infinity and the number pi.

Now you take Stone Mountain and a robin redbreast.
Now say that a robin redbreast was to fly over Stone Mountain every morning, carrying a worm. And as that little feathery bird went over the top, it brushed that hu-u-u-u-uge mound of rock ever so slightly with that little slimy dead worm. Now just try to imagine how long it would take that little robin redbreast to wear down that big hard mountain to the flatness of a parking lot!

Well, now. Along about then, that would just be suppertime (not that you'd get any supper) of your very first day in hell.

From Elements of Story, by Francis Flaherty, quoting an essay written by Roy Blount, Jr. In an essay in the New York Times in which a fictional Southern preacher describes eternal hellfire.

Where We Are, by Gerald Locklin

I envy those who live in two places
New York, say and London, Wales and Spain,
Florida and Chicago -
Hawaii and Switzerland.
There is always the anticipation of the change,
the chance that what is wrong is the result of where you are.
I have always loved both the freshness of arriving and

the relief of leaving.
With two homes every move would be a homecoming.
I am not even considering the weather,
hot or cold, dry or wet:
I am talking about hope.

The mind I love must have wild places, a tangled orchard where
dark damsons drop in the heavy grass, an overgrown little wood,
the chance of a snake or two, a pool that nobody's fathomed the
depth of, and paths threaded with flowers planted by the mind.

Katherine Mansfield

To make a prairie it takes a clover and one bee,
One clover, and a bee,
And revery.
The revery alone will do,
if bees are few.
        Emily Dickenson

Imagination:

What if you slept?

And what if,

In your sleep

You dreamed?

And what if,

In your dream

You went to heaven

and there plucked

A strange and

Beautiful flower?

And what if,

When you awoke,

You had the flower

In your hand?   Samuel Taylor Colerdge

What is now proved was once only imagin'd. William Blake

Ships at a distance have every man's wish on board. — Zora
Neale Hurston, Their Eyes Were Watching God

If one advances confidently in the direction of his dreams, and
endeavors to live the life which he imagined, he will meet with a
success unexpected in common hours....In proportion as he
simplifies his life the laws of the universe will appear less
complex, and solitude will not be solitude, nor poverty poverty,
nor weakness weakness. If you have built castles in the air, your
work need not be lost; that is where they should be. Now put
foundations under them.   Dream and Reality
Henry David Thoreau

Only as high s I reach can I grow
Only as far as I seek can I go,
Only as deep as I look can I see,
Only as much as I dream can I be.
Karen Ravn

The Kiss

I HOPED that he would love me,
And he has kissed my mouth,
But I am like a stricken bird
That cannot reach the south.
For though I know he loves me,
To-night my heart is sad;
His kiss was not so wonderful
As all the dreams I had.
Sara Teasdale

Hope is the thing with feathers
That perches in the soul
And sings the tune without the words
And never stops at all.

— Emily Dickinson

To unpathed waters, undreamed shores. Shakespeare (The Winter's Tale)

The world of reality has its bounds, the world of imagination is boundless; as we cannot enlarge the one, let us restrict the other; for all the sufferings which really make us miserable arise from the difference between the real and the imaginary. Rousseau, Emile, II

When the first baby laughed for the first time, the laugh broke into a thousand pieces and they all went skipping about, and that was the beginning of fairies. And now when every new baby is born its first laugh becomes a fairy. So there ought to be one fairy for every boy or girl. James Matthew Barrie, Peter Pan

---

I cannot tell you how happy I am to have taken up drawing again. I've been thinking about it but always considered the thing impossible and beyond my reach. Vincent Van Gogh

---

[For the next time you say, "Wow, that's big!"]

If the sun were the volume of a watermelon, the earth would lie 140 feet away--and you would need a microscope to see it.

The distance from the earth's surface to its core is 4000 miles. The distance from the sun's surface to its core is 310,000 miles.

Traveling at the speed of light, your voice from *the moon* (voice signals via cellphones travel at the speed of light) would take 1 second to reach Earth;

From the sun, it would take 8 minutes and 20 seconds.

But from the star that is the second closest to Earth (after the Sun, Proxima Centauri) that same signal would take *4 years and 2 months.*

Again, that would be the star that is the *second* closest to the earth.

From the Universe in Your Hand, by Christophe Gilfard

Language

Eloquence is like magic. You have no idea how the trick is done, but you love it. Still, you sense that the magician has worked very hard to make it seem it easy. And she has.

Hearing the right language at the right time is like looking into the right eyes at the right time . . . in the right room.

Language: Most powerful when you read or hear your own thoughts in others' exalted words.

I love the fact that the phrase "to make a long story short " is never timely, and almost always signals a warning that a much longer story is in store. The fairest translation would be "to make a long story—so far, inartfully told—much longer."

The limits of my language mean the limits of my world. Ludwig Wittgenstein

---

By words the mind is winged. Aristophanes, The Birds

"We make out of the quarrel with others, rhetoric, but of the quarrel with ourselves, poetry. "William Butler Yeats
The Discovery of Poetry, Frances Mayes

This, therefore, is the praise of Shakespeare, that his drama is the mirror of life; that he who has mazed his imagination in following the phantoms which other writers raise up before him may here be cured of his delicious ecstasies by reading human sentiments in human language, by scenes from which a hermit may estimate the transactions of the world and a confessor predict the progress of the passions. Dr. Samuel Johnson, Preface to Shakespeare

---

The Sound on the page. Style and Voice in Writing, by Ben Yagoda,

In quoting Judith Thurman, "One of my favorite quotes is from Flaubert: 'As if the soul's fullness didn't sometimes overflow into the emptiest of metaphors, for no one, ever, can give the exact measure of his needs, his apprehensions or his sorrows; and human speech is like a cracked cauldron on which we bang out tunes that make bears dance, when we want to move the stars to pity.' A great sentence is always about what you couldn't say."

Don't tell me the moon is shining; show me the glint of light on broken glass. ~Anton Chekhov

The English language owes a great debt to Shakespeare. He invented over 1700 of our common words by changing nouns into verbs, changing verbs into adjectives, connecting words never before used together, adding prefixes and suffixes, and devising words wholly original. Below is a list of a few of the words Shakespeare coined:
Academe, accused, addiction, advertising, amazement arouse, assassination, backing, bandit, bedroom, beached, besmirch, birthplace, blanket, bloodstained, barefaced, blushing, bet, bump, buzzer, caked, cater, champion, circumstantial. cold-blooded, compromise, courtship, countless, critic, dauntless,

dawn, deafening, discontent, dishearten, drugged, dwindle, epileptic, equivocal, elbow, excitement, exposure, eyeball, fashionable, fixture, flawed, frugal, generous, gloomy, gossip, green-eyed, gust, hint, hobnob, hurried, impede, impartial, invulnerable, jaded, label, lackluster, laughable, lonely, lower, luggage, lustrous, madcap, majestic, marketable, metamorphize, mimic, monumental, moonbeam, mountaineer, negotiate, noiseless, obscene, obsequiously, ode, Olympian, outbreak, panders, pedant, premeditated, puking, radiance, rant, remorseless, savagery, scuffle, secure, skim milk, submerge, summit, swagger, torture. Tranquil, undress, unreal, varied, vaulting, worthless, zany

Shakespeare also invented many of the most-used expressions in our language. Bernard Levin skillfully summarizes Shakespeare's impact in the following passage from The Story of English:

If you cannot understand my argument, and declare "It's Greek to me", you are quoting Shakespeare; if you claim to be more sinned against than sinning, you are quoting Shakespeare; if you recall your salad days, you are quoting Shakespeare; if you act more in sorrow than in anger, if your wish is father to the thought, if your lost property has vanished into thin air, you are quoting Shakespeare; if you have ever refused to budge an inch or suffered from green-eyed jealousy, if you have played fast and loose, if you have been tongue-tied, a tower of strength, hoodwinked or in a pickle, if you have knitted your brows, made a virtue of necessity, insisted on fair play, slept not one wink, stood on ceremony, danced attendance (on your lord and master), laughed yourself into stitches, had short shrift, cold comfort or too much of a good thing, if you have seen better days or lived in a fool's paradise - why, be that as it may, the more fool you, for it is a foregone conclusion that you are (as good luck would have it) quoting Shakespeare; if you think it is early days and clear out bag and baggage, if you think it is high time and that that is the long and short of it, if you believe that the game is up and that truth will out even if it involves your own flesh and blood, if you lie low till the crack of doom because you suspect foul play, if

you have your teeth set on edge (at one fell swoop) without
rhyme or reason, then - to give the devil his due - if the truth
were known (for surely you have a tongue in your head) you are
quoting Shakespeare; even if you bid me good riddance and send
me packing, if you wish I were dead as a door-nail, if you think I
am an eyesore, a laughing stock, the devil incarnate, a stony-
hearted villain, bloody-minded or a blinking idiot, then - by
Jove! O Lord! Tut, tut! for goodness' sake! what the dickens! but
me no buts - it is all one to me, for you are quoting Shakespeare.
(Bernard Levin. From The Story of English. Robert McCrum,
William Cran and Robert MacNeil. Viking

By telling stories, you objectify your own experience. You
separate it from yourself. You pin down certain truths. You
make up others. You start sometimes with an incident that truly
happened, like the night in the shit field, and you carry it forward
by inventing incidents that did not in fact occur but that
nonetheless help to clarify and explain. Tim O'Brien, The
Things They Carried.

Listen. But not too closely, since what I'm saying is not exactly
what I mean.

James Richardson

"I may not be persuaded by Emersonianism as an ideology, but
Emerson—his voice, his language, his music—persuades me. . . .
I may regard (or discard) the idea of the soul as no better then a
puff of warm vapor, But here is Emerson on the soul: 'When it
breathes through [man's] intellect, it is genius; when it breathes
through his will, it is virtue; when it flows through his affection,
it is love.' And then—well, I am in thrall; I am possessed; I
believe."

Explaining that trust in the author and disagreement with the author can coexist In an essay about essays—"She: Portrait of the Essay as a Warm Body"—Cynthia Ozick describes her experience of reading Emerson.

Steve Martin: Some people have a way with words, and other people, oh, uh, not have way.

Story of two Trappist monks:
Monk 1 asks his abbot if it would be alright if he smoked while he prayed. Scandalized, the abbot said, "Of course not. That borders on sacrilege."
Monk 2 asked his abbot whether it would be alright if he prayed while he smoked. "Of course," said the abbot, "God wants to hear from us at any time."

"Mindware, Tools for smart Thinking," by Richard NIsbett

When Aeschines spoke, the people said, "How well he speaks."
But when Demosthenes spoke, they said, "Let us march!"
Unknown

We don't read and write poetry because it's cute. We read and write poetry because we are members of the human race. And the human race is filled with passion. And medicine, law, business, engineering, these are noble pursuits and necessary to sustain life. But poetry, beauty, romance, these are what we stay alive for.   Dead Poet's Society

---

Poetry strips the veil of familiarity from things. Shelley

Life

It's a carnival where you don't get to pick the rides, except for the roller coaster. And, anytime you want, you can step up and take a chance for that teddy bear. Usually, the teddy bear is safe.

Life: The passing of miracles, masked as mundane.

Everyone we meet is a mentor. Live as if this were true.

Let Me Be . . .

The Love, *that is the verb—an action, a behavior—that leads to a love-filled* feeling, *in both the lover and the loved.*

The Forgiveness, *that begins the escape from the unhappy place that others have built for me to live.*

The Journey, *that leads me to challenge, that leads me to discovery, that leads me to change, that leads me to me.*

The Teacher, *that finds the questions the student needs to find his own answers.*

The Determined, *that softens the rains, quiets the winds and sees all things as possible.*

The Contentedness, *that comes not simply from having owned it, but from having actually earned it.*

The Good, *that shows itself not in the absence of mistakes* *made, but in the deliberate effort to make a positive difference in the worlds that I touch.*

The Question, *that marries the good answer.*

The Smile, *that others capture, and hold on to, for times when they need it most.*

The Story, *that inspires others to tell their own stories, and to live them.*

The Intellect, *that is sufficient to understand that what's most important to be understood needs more than intellect alone.*

The Genuine Apology, *that serves not to rake over rough roads, but to pave new and better ones.*

The Magic, *that leads to preparation . . . that leads to the magic.*

The Student, *who sees far enough to see the bend—but only the bend— and who appreciates the need to move forward to discover for himself what lies beyond it.*

The Challenge, *that moves me day to day to the edge of my abilities.*

The Courage, *that I might live the fullness of my potential.*

The Gratitude, *that is thankful for the times my mind and heart have danced together.*

The Lessons, *that my mistakes in life have brought to me— that I might not only pass them on, but also live them.*

The Imagination, *that surprises even my self, and unbinds* *the ribbons of a better life.*

The Person, *that only I can be, and the one that finds the very best that can be found inside of me.*

If you're not thankful for now, be thankful for then—Now will change.

Everyman

One man after another came to him for advice.
And he listened.
And, as he listened, they spoke more.
And he listened more.
And, in his listening, they found their answers.

And then he sought for someone . . .

To listen to *him*

Times of a Life
If I could choose
one minute, one hour, a day
a week, a month
and a year of my life,
which minute, which moment,
which times would I choose?

It is the nature of years
that make them vulnerable;
their very last days stand as ready as their first to speak for their
entireties.

One could never say, for example,
"It was a great year,
although my child died that year."

Yes, years are difficult.
Sometimes they fool you, starting out well,
yet while the weeks become months
a change will come, surely,
and that year—because of one insurmountable change—
will no longer be in the running.

So I would look for a year without fireworks
or frenzy, without death or deceit,
without sickness or sanctimony.
I would look for a year with peace,
with growth, with learning, with health
and with self-respect.
My year would flood with family and friends,
with love, with memories.

My month would include sacrifice,
perseverance and commitment
at levels too high to endure for a year.

My week would have beaches and books,
cities and countries unknown,
exploration, observation, and a return
to a home
where favorable comparisons can be made,
however good the week.

My day would be with family and friends
who make a day seem too short.

An hour would be with my love,
My beautiful wife,
a portion allocated to anticipation,

to hope, to her eyes,

leading to One Minute (less of course)
—One glorious shortened minute,
near the end of the hour.

Ten Suggestions (that may lead to a better day.)

1. Remember that you are never as good as you think you are, or as bad.
2. Remember this about everyone else too.
3. Don't reject things that are "counter-intuitive." Nobody ever said intuition was perfect.
4. Whenever you think you can accomplish something, prove yourself right.
5. Once a day let your "child" out to play.
6. Act as if only you are responsible for your memories.
7. Live as if others' mistakes, sins, faults, crimes—even arrogance—were simply there to remind you that you've got a few problems too.
8. Tell somebody you like them, and hope you've already made it obvious.
9. Think of the best thing about your mother, the best thing about your father, or anyone else who has touched you in your life, and remember that it's you who recognizes and loves that goodness, and it's you whom they have touched.
10. Think of forgiveness as a game in which you make all the rules, but that those rules will ultimately be used to determine whether *you* are forgiven.

BONUS: Pick one suggestion (or more), and make it a

commandment.

He was an old man, and he was often angry at those closest to them.

"You need to change!" he would say.

And they wouldn't change.

And then, he heard, for the first time,

in his own voice,

"*I* am the one who needs to change."

And he did,

And when he changed,

soon after

he noticed

that those others

seemed to change as well.

The first step is to put them all in an imagined room—the regrets, the mistakes, the should-haves, the could-haves and the would-haves—and lock them away.

But here's the second step, because locks mean little to us if we hold the keys:

Imagine your lock is a *combination* lock.

But not just any combination lock—

Here's the third step: this combination lock needs you to twist and turn its dial 100 times before it unlocks.

At right around 50, you will find yourself saying, "Is this

really worth it?"

And the room will stay locked.

And you will move on to a better use of your time.

It is after the commas, the periods, and the exclamation points of our lives that we grow,

but it is after the question marks that we determine how *well* we grow.

Family

I yelled
because I knew I was losing.
Not that I was losing the argument;
I don't care about arguments.
I yelled because I knew I was losing family,
because parts of my family were broken,
and no one, not even I,
the husband and father, the son and the brother,
could
help.
After I yelled, I cried,
alone.

The reasons you lose family aren't important,
unless you know it is the judge in you
that made the ruling,
and you know
that you don't know
the truth

about anything
having to do with the
caring, loving,
humans,
humans,
whom we all call family

and you live with that uncertainty,
not only of the facts,
but of who you are -
who the Hell you are -
to have allowed anyone
to pick apart those pieces
that needed help.

Let each of us now, separately,
find solace in our separate stories,
hoping that it is we who will tell them,
for only then will anyone hear our truth,
if they care enough to listen,
and only then, by our repetition,
can we remember
the reasons why
our family is smaller
than the one we were given.
God knows, when we seek forgiveness,
if we are given the opportunity to tell our story
we will need to remember
and explain well
the reasons why.

Sometimes you win and sometimes you learn.

      Robert Kiyosaki, author of Rich Dad, Poor Dad

Not a shred of evidence exists in favor of the idea that life is serious, though it is often hard and even terrible. And saying that, I am prompted to add what follows out of it; that since everything ends badly for us, in the inescapable catastrophe of death, it seems obvious that the first rule of life is to have a good time; and that the second rule of life is to hurt as few people as possible in the course of doing so. There is no third rule. New Yorker writer Brendan Gill

---

Dalai Lama's 18 rules for living

1. Take into account that great love and great achievements involve great risk.
2. When you lose, don't lose the lesson.
3. Follow the three Rs:
    1. Respect for self
    2. Respect for others
    3. Responsibility for all your actions.
4. Remember that not getting what you want is sometimes a wonderful stroke of luck.
5. Learn the rules so you know how to break them properly
6. Don't let a little dispute injure a great friendship.
7. When you realize you've made a mistake, take immediate steps to correct it.
8. Spend some time alone every day.
9. Open your arms to change, but don't let go of your values.
10. Remember that silence is sometimes the best answer.
11. Live a good, honorable life. Then when you get older and think back, you'll be able to enjoy it a second time.
12. A loving atmosphere in your home is the foundation for your life.
13. In disagreements with loved ones, deal only with the current situation. Don't bring up the past.

14. Share your knowledge. It's a way to achieve
    immortality.
15. Be gentle with the earth.
16. Once a year, go someplace you've never been
    before.
17. Remember that the best relationship is one in
    which your love for each other exceeds your need for
    each other.
18. Judge your success by what you had to give up in
    order to get it.

Into my heart an air that kills

 From yon far country blows:

What are those blue remembered hills,

 What spires, what farms are those?

That is the land of lost content,

 I see it shining plain,

The happy highways where I went

 And cannot come again.

A.E. Houseman, A Shropshire Lad

I would rather be ashes than dust! I would rather that my spark
burn out in a brilliant blaze than it be stifled by dry-rot. I would
rather be a superb meteor, every atom of me in magnificent glow,
than a sleepy and permanent planet. Jack London

Do any human beings ever realize life while they live it? —every,
every minute? Our Town, Thornton Wilder

The past is a foreign country; they do things differently there.
L.P. Hartley's novel The Go-Between

"Life is a game, boy. Life is a game that one plays according to the rules."

"Yes, sir. I know it is. I know it."

"Game, my ass. Some game. If you get on the side where all the hot-shots are, then it's a game, all right – I'll admit that. But if you get on the other side, where there aren't any hot-shots, then what's a game about it. Nothing. No game."

Holden Caulfield in The Catcher In The Rye, J.D. Salinger

I been silent so long now it's gonna roar out of me like floodwaters and you think the guy telling this is ranting and raving my God; you think this is too horrible to have really happened, this is too awful to be the truth! But, please. It's still hard for me to have a clear mind thinking on it. But it's the truth even if it didn't happen.

One Flew Over the Cuckoo's Nest, Ken Kesey

Within the hour I'll land, and strangely enough I'm in no hurry to have it pass. I haven't the slightest desire to sleep. There's not an ache in my body. The night is cool and safe. I want to sit quietly in this cockpit and let the realization of my completed flight sink in....

It's like struggling up a mountain after a rare flower, and then, when you have it within arm's reach, realizing that satisfaction and happiness lie more in the finding than the plucking. Plucking and withering are inseparable....

I almost wish Paris were a few more hours away. It's a shame to land with the night so clear and so much fuel in my tanks.

Charles Lindbergh near the end of his 1927 solo flight across the Atlantic.

[W]hen they were not arguing, the boredom was so fierce that one day the old woman ventured to say: - I should like to know which is worse, being raped a hundred times by negro pirates, having a buttock cut off, running the gauntlet in the Bulgar army, being flogged and hanged in an auto-da-fe, being dissected and rowing in the galleys – experiencing, in a word, all the miseries through which we have passed – or else just sitting here and doing nothing. –It's a hard question, said Candide. These words gave rise to new reflections, and Martin in particular concluded that man was bound to live either in convulsions of misery or in the lethargy of boredom.
Candide discuss whether misery or boredom is better. Candide, by Voltaire

---

A son and his father were walking on the mountains. Suddenly, his son falls, hurts himself and screams:
"AAAhhhhhhhhhhhhhh!!!"
To his surprise, he hears the voice repeating, somewhere in the mountain: "AAAhhhhhhhhhhhhhh!!!"
Curious, he yells: "Who are you?"
He receives the answer: "Who are you?"
Angered at the response, he screams: "Coward!"
He receives the answer: "Coward!"
He looks to his father and asks: "What's going on?"
The father smiles and says: "My son, pay attention."
And then he screams to the mountain: "I admire you!"
The voice answers: "I admire you!"
Again the man screams: "You are a champion!"
The voice answers: "You are a champion!"

The boy is surprised, but does not understand.

Then the father explains: "People call this ECHO, but really this is LIFE. It gives you back everything you say or do. Our life is simply a reflection of our actions. If you want more love in the world, create more love in your heart. If you want more competence in your team, improve your competence. This relationship applies to everything, in all aspects of life; life will give you back everything you have given to it."

YOUR LIFE IS NOT A COINCIDENCE. IT'S A REFLECTION OF YOU!

(Source Unknown)

The world's greatest geniuses have all had 24 personality characteristics in common and you can develop the same traits yourself, says an expert. "Most people have the mistaken idea that geniuses are born, not made", declared clinical psychologist Dr. Alfred Barrious, founder and director of the Self-Programmed Control Center of Los Angeles and author of the book, Towards Greater Freedom and Happiness.

"But if you look at the lives of the worlds greatest geniuses like Edison, Socrates, DaVinci, Shakespeare, Einstein, you will discover they all had 24 personality characteristics in common. These are traits that anyone can develop. It makes no difference how old you are, how much education you have, or what you have accomplished to date. Adopting these personality characteristics enables you to operate on a genius level." Here are the Characteristics Dr. Barrios lists, which enable geniuses to come up with and develop new and fruitful ideas: 1. DRIVE. Geniuses have a strong desire to work hard and long. They're willing to give all they've got to a project. Develop your drive by focusing on your future success, and keep going. 2. COURAGE. It takes courage to do things others consider impossible. Stop worrying about what people will think if you're different.   3. DEVOTION TO GOALS. Geniuses know what they want and go after it. Get control of your life and schedule. Have something specific to accomplish each day.   4. KNOWLEDGE. Geniuses continually accumulate information. Never go to sleep at night without having learned at least one new thing each day. Read. And question people who know.   5. HONESTY. Geniuses are frank, forthright and honest. Take the responsibility for thins that go wrong. Be willing to admit, 'I goofed' and learned from my mistakes.   6. OPTIMISM. Geniuses never doubt they will succeed. Deliberately focus your mind on something good coming up.   7. ABILITY TO JUDGE. Try to understand the facts of a situation before you judge. Evaluate things on an opened minded, unprejudiced basis and be willing to change your mind.   8. ENTHUSIASM. Geniuses are so excited about what they are doing, it encourages others to cooperate with them. Really believe that things will out well. Don't hold back.   9. WILLINGNESS TO TAKE CHANCES. Overcome your fear of failure. You won't be afraid to take chances once you realize you can learn from your mistakes.   10. DYNAMIC ENERGY. Don't sit on your butt waiting for something good to happen. Be determined to make it happen. 11. ENTERPRISE. Geniuses are opportunity seekers. Be willing to take on jobs others won't touch. Never be afraid to try the unknown.   12. PERSUASION. Geniuses know how to motivate people to help them get ahead. You'll find it easy to be persuasive if you believe in what you're doing.   13. OUTGOINGNESS. I've found geniuses able to make friends easily and be easy on their friends. Be a 'booster' not somebody who puts others down. That attitude will win you many valuable friends.   14. ABILITY TO COMMUNICATE. Geniuses are generally able to get their ideas across to others. Take every opportunity to explain your ideas to others.   15. PATIENCE. Be patient with others most of the time, but always be impatient with your self. Expect far more of yourself than others.   16. PERCEPTION. Geniuses have their mental radar working full time. Think more of others' needs and wants than you do your own.   17. PERFECTIONISM. Geniuses cannot tolerate mediocrity, particularly in themselves. Never be easily satisfied with your self. Always strive to do better. 18. SENSE OF HUMOR. Be willing to laugh at your own expense. Don't take offense when the joke is on you. 19. VERSATILITY. The more things you learn to accomplish, the more confidence you will develop. Don't shy away from new endeavors. 20. ADAPTABILITY. Being flexible enables you to adapt to changing circumstances readily. Resist doing things the same old way. Be willing to consider new options. 21. CURIOSITY. An inquisitive, curious mind will help you seek out new information. Don't be afraid to admit you don't know it all. Always ask questions about things you don't understand. 22. INDIVIDUALISM. Do things the way you think they should be done, without fearing somebody's disapproval. 23. IDEALISM. Keep your feet on the ground -- but have your head in the clouds. Strive to achieve great things, not just for yourself but for the better of mankind. 24. IMAGINATION. Geniuses know how to think in new combinations, see things from a different perspective, than anyone else. Unclutter your mental environment to develop this type of imagination. Give yourself time each day to daydream, to fantasize, to drift into a dreamy inner life the way you did as a child

---

In the end, it's not going to matter how many breaths you took, but how many moments took your breath away.

 shing xiong

E.L. Doctorow said once said that "Writing a novel is like driving a car at night. You can see only as far as your headlights, but you can make the whole trip that way. You don't have to see where you're going, you don't have to see your destination or everything you will pass along the way. You just have to see two or three feet ahead of you." This is right up there with the best advice on writing, or life, I have ever heard.

Begin. Open. *Anywhere.*

— Anne Lamott (Bird by Bird: Some Instructions on Writing and Life)

After awhile you learn
the subtle difference between
holding a hand and chaining a soul
and you learn that love doesn't mean possession
and company doesn't mean security.
And you begin to learn that kisses aren't contracts
and presents aren't promises and you begin to accept
your defeats with your head up and your eyes ahead
with the grace of an adult not the grief of a child.
And you learn to build your roads today
because tomorrow's ground is too uncertain for plans
and futures have ways of falling down in mid-flight.
After awhile you learn that even sunshine
burns if you get too much so you plant your
own garden and decorate your own soul
instead of waiting for someone to bring you flowers.
And you learn that you really can endure
that you really are strong
and you really do have worth
and you learn
and you learn...
Robert Herrick

Autobiography in Five Short Chapters
by Portia Nelson

> I. I walk down the street.
>   There's a deep hole in the sidewalk.
>   I fall in.
>   I am lost.....I am helpless;
>   it isn't my fault.
> It takes forever to find a way out.

II. I walk down the same street.
　　There is a deep hole in the sidewalk.
　　I pretend I don't see it.
　　I fall in again.
　　I can't believe I am in the same place;
　　　　but it isn't my fault.
It still takes a long time to get out.

III. I walk down the same street.
　　There is a deep hole in the sidewalk.
　　I see it is there.
　　I still fall in....it's a habit.
　　　　My eyes are open.
　　　　I know where I am.
It is my fault.
I get out immediately.

IV. I walk down the same street.
　　There is a deep hole in the sidewalk.
　　I walk around it.

V. I walk down a different street.

Lessons From Geese

Fact 1: As each goose flaps its wings it creates an "uplift" for the birds that follow. By flying in a "V" formation, the whole flock adds 71% greater flying range than if each bird flew alone. Lesson 1: People who share a common direction and sense of community can get where they are going quicker and easier because they are traveling on the thrust of one another.

Fact 2: When a goose falls out of formation, it suddenly feels the drag and resistance of flying alone. It quickly moves back into formation to take advantage of the lifting power of the bird in front of it.

Lesson 2: If we have as much common sense as a goose, we stay in formation with those headed where we want to go. We are willing to accept their help and give our help to others.

Fact 3: When the lead goose tires, it rotates back into the formation and another goose flies to the point position. Lesson 3: It pays to take turns doing the hard tasks and sharing leadership. As with geese, people are interdependent on each other's skills, capabilities, and unique arrangements of gifts, talents, or resources.

Fact 4: Geese flying in formation honk to encourage those up front to keep up their speed.

Lesson 4: We need to make sure our honking is encouraging. In groups where there is encouragement, the production is much greater. The power of encouragement (to stand by one's heart or core values and encourage the heart and core of others) is the quality of honking we seek. Fact 5: When a goose gets sick, wounded, or shot down, two geese drop out of formation and follow it down to help protect it. They stay with it until it dies or is able to fly again. Then, they launch out with another formation or catch up with the flock.

Lesson 5: If we have as much sense as geese, we will stand by each other in difficult times as well as when we are strong. -- From Christine Hill

---

The Six Mistakes of Man

The illusion that personal gain is made up of crushing others

The tendency to worry about things that cannot be changed or corrected

Insisting that a thing is impossible because we cannot accomplish it

Refusing to set aside trivial preferences

Neglecting development and refinement of the mind and not
acquiring the habit of reading and study
Attempting to compel others to believe and live as we do. Cicero
(106-43 BC)

Though nothing can bring back the hour
Of splendour in the grass, of glory in the flower
        Ode: Intimations of Immortality From Recollections of
Early Childhood.

Laws of Success
 Do you want something? -- Will you pay the price? The great
sin -- Gossip. The great crippler -- Fear. The greatest mistake --
Giving up. The most satisfying experience -- Doing your duty
first. The best action -- Keep the mind clear and judgment good.
The greatest blessing -- Good health. The biggest fool - The man
who lies to himself. The great gamble -- Substituting hope for
facts. The most certain thing in life -- Change. The greatest joy
-- Being needed. The cleverest man -- The one who does what
he thinks is right. The most potent force -- Positive thinking.
The greatest opportunity -- The next one. The greatest thought --
God. The greatest victory -- Victory over self. The best play --
Successful work. The greatest handicap -- Egotism. The most
expensive indulgence -- Hate. The most dangerous man -- The
liar The most ridiculous trait -- False pride. The greatest loss --
Loss of self confidence. The greatest need -- Common sense.

"If" by Rudyard Kipling

If you can keep your head when all about you
Are losing theirs and blaming it on you;

If you can trust yourself when all men doubt you,
But make allowance for their doubting too;
If you can wait and not be tired by waiting,
Or being lied about, don't deal in lies,
Or being hated, don't give way to hating,
And yet don't look too good, nor talk too wise;

If you can dream - and not make dreams your master;
If you can think - and not make thoughts your aim;
If you can meet with Triumph and Disaster
And treat those two imposters just the same;
If you can bear to hear the truth you've spoken
Twisted by knaves to make a trap for fools,
Or watch the things you gave your life to, broken,
And stoop and build 'em up with worn-out tools;

If you can make one heap of all your winnings
And risk it on one turn of pitch-and-toss,
And lose, and start again at your beginnings
And never breathe a word about your loss;
If you can force your heart and nerve and sinew
To serve your turn long after they are gone,
And so hold on when there is nothing in you
Except the Will which says to them: "Hold on!"

If you can talk with crowds and keep your virtue,
Or walk with Kings - nor lose the common touch,
If neither foes nor loving friends can hurt you,
If all men count with you, but none too much;
If you can fill the unforgiving minute
With sixty seconds' worth of distance run,
Yours is the Earth and everything that's in it,
And - which is more - you'll be a man, my son!

Over the years many people have offered their models of the
"Good Life", and some have left quotes that nicely summarize

important truths. The following are ten of my personal favorites.

1.Know Thyself — Socrates. From ancient Greece comes this reminder that introspection, keeping a journal, paying attention to the heart of things, comes first. Before we can know the world around us, and make wise choices, we must first come to grips with who we are and what we value.

2.To Thine Own Self Be True — Shakespeare. In life there is no substitute for integrity. My grandmother was fond of saying, "We either stand for something, or we'll fall for anything." Integrity is about going beyond the truth to full and complete honesty, openness and fairness.

3.And the Greatest of These is Love — St Paul. He also observed that "without love I am just a clanging symbol or a noisy gong." Without love, caring relationships, and compassion, life is indeed a dry and shallow thing.

4.Imagination Rules the World — Albert Einstein. The good life is at least partly based on dreams that are worthy of us, dreams that elevate and challenge and inspire our best. Bobby Kennedy noted, "Others look at the world and ask, 'Why?' I dream of a world that never was and ask, 'Why not?'" Martin Luther King's defiant cry, "I have a dream!" will live long after most of us are gone and forgotten.

5.Too much of a good thing is just right — Mae West. The good life is about living large, about expressing the joy and love of life. It's about song, exuberance, and about taking chances, and "going for it".

6.Opportunities multiply as they are seized — Sun Tzu. Success depends on the courage to act, and courage in turn requires a level of faith that every opportunity acted upon will lead to more and better ways to serve, learn, grow and prosper.

7.Do, or do not. There is no "try". — Yoda (The Empire Strikes Back). Life requires action, boldness and decisiveness. Mae West also observed, "He who hesitates is a damned fool."

8.Perfection is achieved, not when there is nothing left to add, but when there is nothing left to take away — Antoine de St. Exupery. Henry Thoreau recommended, "Simplify, simplify, simplify. Let your concerns be as 2 or 3, not more." Friends, work, the media and this thing called the Internet, along with our own "wish lists" try to seduce us to complexity, busy-ness and anxiety. Keep it simple!

9.The artist is nothing without gift, but gift is nothing without work — Emile Zola. Only focused, intelligent, diligent effort turns potential into reality. Without creative effort, talent and "gift" seem to atrophy and die. Truly a case of "use it or lose it".

10.There are two ways to live your life. One is as though nothing is a miracle. The other is as though everything is a miracle. — Albert Einstein.

I highly recommend practicing the attitude of gratitude. What else is there? -- by Philip E. Humbert, PhD, a Psychologist, Personal Coach and entrepreneur.

"If I Had My Life to Live Over"

If I had my life to live over again,
 I would try to make more mistakes next time...
 I'd try not to be so damned perfect;
 I'd relax more, I'd limber up,
 I'd be sillier than I've been on this trip;
 In fact, I know of very few things I'd take quite so seriously;
 I'd be crazier ... and I'd certainly be less hygienic;
 I'd take more chances ... I'd take more trips ...
 I'd climb more mountains ... I'd swim more rivers ...
 And I'd watch more sunsets;
 I'd burn more gasoline,
 I'd eat more ice cream - and fewer beans;
 I'd have more actual troubles and fewer imaginary ones,

 You see, I was one of those people who lived prophylactically and sensibly,

hour-after-hour and day-after-day;
Oh, that doesn't mean I didn't have my moments,
But if I had it to do all over, I'd have more of those moments,
In fact, I'd try to have nothing but wonderful moments, side-by-side.

I was one of those people who never went anywhere without a thermometer,
a hot water bottle, a gargle, a raincoat and a parachute;
If I had it to do all over again, I'd travel lighter next time.

If I had my life to live all over again,
I'd start barefoot earlier in the spring
and I'd stay that way later in the fall;
I'd play hooky a lot more;
I'd ride more merry-go-rounds, I'd pick more flowers,
I'd hug more children,
I'd tell more people that I loved them,
If I had my life to live over again;
But, you see, I don't.

by Nadine Staff, (age 85), Louisville, Kentucky

Laugh, and the world laughs with you;
Weep, and you weep alone.
For the sad old earth must borrow its mirth,
But has trouble enough of its own.
Sing, and the hills will answer;
Sigh, it is lost on the air.
The echoes bound to a joyful sound,
But shrink from voicing care.

Rejoice, and men will seek you;
Grieve, and they turn and go.
They want full measure of all your pleasure,
But they do not need your worry.

Be glad, and your friends are many;
Be sad, and you lose them all.
There are none to decline your nectared wine,
But alone you must drink life's gall.

Feast, and your halls are crowded;
Fast, and the world goes by.
Succeed and give, and it helps you live,

but no man can help you die.
There is room in the halls of pleasure
For a long and lordly train,
But one by one we must all file on
Through the narrow aisles of pain.   Ella Wheeler Wilcox

Ithaka by Constantine P. Cavafy

As you set out for Ithaka
hope your road is a long one,
full of adventure, full of discovery.
Laistrygonians, Cyclops,
angry Poseidon-don't be afraid of them:
you'll never find things like that on your way
as long as you keep your thoughts raised high,
as long as a rare excitement
stirs your spirit and your body.
Laistrygonians, Cyclops,
wild Poseidon-you won't encounter them
unless you bring them along inside your soul,
unless your soul sets them up in front of you.

Hope your road is a long one.

May there be many summer mornings when,
with what pleasure, what joy,
you enter harbors you're seeing for the first time;
may you stop at Phoenician trading stations
to buy fine things,
mother of pearl and coral, amber and ebony,
sensual perfume of every kind-
as many sensual perfumes as you can;
and may you visit many Egyptian cities
to learn and go on learning from their scholars.

Keep Ithaka always in your mind.
Arriving there is what you're destined for.
But don't hurry the journey at all.
Better if it lasts for years,
so you're old by the time you reach the island,
wealthy with all you've gained on the way,
not expecting Ithaka to make you rich.
Ithaka gave you the marvelous journey.
Without her you wouldn't have set out.
She has nothing left to give you now.

And if you find her poor, Ithaka won't have fooled you.
Wise as you will have become, so full of experience,
you'll have understood by then what these Ithakas mean.

What a great poem! You can see yourself fighting them all to get
there; the Laistrygonians, the Cyclops, every pain, every setback,
every disappointment. Through it all, our Ithaka waits for us so
solidly that we can endure and grow from the twists and turns
that life affords us on the way, and yet it's a city we may never
reach.

 Still, it will have served its purpose; it will have enriched our
lives, given us the hope necessary to persevere and maybe, just
maybe, it will have allowed us to stumble upon our own places
of peace along the way.

This poem received a lot of attention in 1971 when it was taken to the moon by astronaut James B. Irwin on Apollo 15. Irwin's mother gave it to him before the flight and he actually left a copy of the poem on the moon.

The author, James Dillet Freeman, is poet laureate of the Unity School of Christianity at Unity Village. He wrote the poem in 1947.

Prayer of St. Francis

Lord, make me an instrument of your Peace.
Where there is hatred, let me sow love.
Where there is injury, pardon.
Where there is doubt, faith.
Where there is despair, hope.
Where there is darkness, light.
Where there is sadness, joy!

O Divine Master,
Grant that I may not so much seek
to be consoled as to console;
To be understood as to understand;
To be loved as to love.

For it is in giving that we receive,
it is in pardoning that we are pardoned,
and it is in dying that we are born to eternal life

It's fitting that St. Francis begins his prayer asking that God make him an Instrument of His peace. By time you finish reading it you realize that its focus is not on the "pray-er" but on anyone other than the pray-er. That shift of focus away from himself ironically gives the pray-er his peace.

There are years that ask questions, and years that answer. Zora Neale Hurston

Story of the Five Balls of life.

Imagine life is a game in which you are juggling five balls. The balls are called work, family, health, friends, and integrity. And you're keeping all of them in the air. But one day you finally come to understand that work is a rubber ball. If you drop it, it will bounce back. The other four balls - family, health, friends, integrity - are made of glass. If you drop one of these, it will be irrevocably scuffed, nicked, perhaps even shattered,. And once you truly understand the lesson of the five balls, you will have the beginnings of balance in your life.

From James Patterson's Suzanne's diary for Nicholas.

As we grow up, we learn that even the one person that wasn't supposed to ever let us down, probably will. You'll have your heart broken and you'll break others' hearts. You'll fight with your best friend or maybe even fall in love with them, and you'll cry because time is flying by. So take too many pictures, laugh too much, forgive freely, and love like you've never been hurt. Life comes with no guarantees, no time outs, no second chances. You just have to live life to the fullest, tell someone what they mean to you and tell someone off, speak out, dance in the pouring rain, hold someone's hand, comfort a friend, fall asleep watching the sun come up, stay up late, be a flirt, and smile until your face hurts. Don't be afraid to take chances or fall in love and most of all, live in the moment because every second you spend angry or upset is a second of happiness you can never get back. - Unknown

Bound to Please by Michael Dirda, an extraordinary one-volume literary education, starts by author saying he enjoys reading history "for what the Greeks called tisis: Fate's assurance that the biter is ultimately bitten and that, in the end comeuppance will be delivered to the overconfident and cruel."

The road is always better than the inn. Cervantes

Tomorrow, and tomorrow, and tomorrow,
Creeps in this petty pace from day to day
To the last syllable of recorded time,
And all our yesterdays have lighted fools
The way to dusty death. Out, out, brief candle!
Life's but a walking shadow, a poor player
That struts and frets his hour upon the stage
And then is heard no more: it is a tale
Told by an idiot, full of sound and fury,
Signifying nothing.
    William Shakespeare, spoken by Macbeth

When sorrows come, they come not single spies, but in battalions.

Shakespeare

A lesson from a Mad Hatter

One of the first steps to accomplishing great things in your life is to cease dwelling on the negative things in your past. Carefully assess your present strengths, successes, and achievements. Dwell on those positive events in your life, and quit limiting your potential by constantly thinking about what you have done poorly. Alice and the Mad Hatter in Wonderland had a conversation that illustrates this concept:

Alice: Where I come from, people study what they are not good at in order to be able to do what they are good at.

Mad Hatter: We only go around in circles in Wonderland, but we always end up where we started. Would you mind explaining yourself?

Alice: Well, grown-ups tell us to find out what we did wrong, and never do it again.

Mad Hatter: That's odd! It seems to me that in order to find out about something, you have to study it. And when you study it, you should become better at it. Why should you want to become better at something and then never do it again? But please continue.

Alice: Nobody ever tells us to study the right things we do. We're only supposed to learn from the wrong things. But we are permitted to study the right things other people do. And sometimes we're even told to copy them.

Mad Hatter: That's cheating!

Alice: You're quite right, Mr. Hatter. I do live in a topsy-turvy world. It seems like I have to do something wrong first, in order to learn from what not to do. And then, by not doing what I'm not supposed to do, perhaps I'll be right. But I'd rather be right the first time, wouldn't you?

". . . sin that pays its way can travel freely, and without a passport; whereas Virtue, if a pauper, is stopped at all frontiers."

Herman Melville, Moby Dick (When Jonas, a suspected sinner, prepays his fare on a ship scheduled to set sail at first tide, later than Jonas had wanted, to discourage any suspicion that he's on the run)

In "Going to Walden," the poet Mary Oliver reflects on the complex "message" of Thoreau. In her poem, she responds to friends who suggest that she drive to Walden Pond for a day trip, to get in touch with the meaning of Thoreau's masterwork. She resists going on this physical journey, suggesting that

> Going to Walden is not so easy a thing
> As a green visit. It is the slow and difficult
> Trick of living, and finding it where you are.

Promised Land, Thirteen Books that Changed America, Jay Parini,

---

Mastery lives quietly atop a mountain of mistakes.

Eric Greitens, Resilience

. . . We should understand that those who have built true excellence in their lives are always fighting at the edges of their ability. Eric Greitens, Resilience

---

A man's Life must be nailed to a cross either of Thought or Action." Winston Churchill (From Churchill's Trial)

Ask yourself, *What is the best I can do?* And then do that.

Brave Enough, Cheryl Strayed

What's important is that you make the leap. Jump high and hard with intention and heart. Pay no mind to the vision that the committee made up. **You get to make your life.**

Brave Enough, Cheryl Strayed

It isn't too late.
Time. Is not running out.
Your life is here and now.
And the moment has arrived
at which you're finally ready
to change.

Brave Enough, Cheryl Strayed

Do not believe that the person who is trying to offer you solace lives his life effortlessly among the simple and quiet words that might occasionally comfort you. His life is filled with much hardship and sadness, and it remains far behind yours. But if it were otherwise, he could never have found these words.
The Wisdom of Rilke

Tom Sawyer: "Hard even on hearing the best preacher on Sunday, to stay saved past Tuesday."

The black belt of presence is to notice when you're not aware.
No Gawdat, Solve for Happy

Who has no chaos inside him will never give birth to a dancing star.

Thus Spoke Zarathustra, Nietzsche

"When my daughter was about seven years old, she asked me one day what I did at work. I told her I worked at the college—that my job was to teach people how to draw. She stared at me, incredulous, and said, 'You mean they forget?'" Howard Ikemoto, from *The Creative License,* by Danny Gregory

---

The bitterest tears shed over graves are for words left unsaid and deeds left undone. Harriet Beecher Stowe.

Atticus said to Jem one day, "I'd rather you shot at tin cans in the backyard, but I know you'll go after birds. Shoot all the blue jays you want, if you can hit 'em, but remember it's a sin to kill a mockingbird." That was the only time I ever heard Atticus say it was a sin to do something, and I asked Miss Maudie about it. "Your father's right," she said. "Mockingbirds don't do one thing except make music for us to enjoy. They don't eat up people's gardens, don't nest in corn cribs, they don't do one thing but sing their hearts out for us. That's why it's a sin to kill a mockingbird. – Harper Lee, To Kill a Mockingbird

---

He allowed himself to be swayed by his conviction that human beings are not born once and for all on the day their mothers give birth to them, but that life obliges them over and over again to

give birth to themselves.
— Gabriel Garcí-a Márquez, Love in the Time of Cholera

"Sometimes I can hear my bones straining under the weight of all the lives I'm not living."- Jonathan Safran Foer, Extremely Loud and Incredibly Close

---

But I tried, didn't I? Goddamnit, at least I did that. – Ken Kesey, One Flew Over the Cuckoo's Nest

---

"We look up at the same stars, and see such different things." – George R.R. Martin, A Storm of Swords

---

There are years that ask questions and years that answer. -Zora Neale Hurston, Their Eyes Were Watching God

---

Today is the youngest you will ever be. Live like it. Mark Cuban, quoting his father, saying it was the best advice he was ever given.

Our deepest fear is not that we are inadequate. Our deepest fear is that we are powerful beyond measure. It is our light, not our darkness that most frightens us. We ask ourselves "Who am I to be brilliant, gorgeous, talented, fabulous?" Actually, who are you not to be? You are a child of God. Your playing small does not serve the world. There is nothing enlightened about shrinking so that other people won't feel insecure around you. We are all meant to shine, as children do. We were born to make manifest the glory of God that is within us. It'/s not just in some of us; it's in everyone. And as we let our own light shine, we unconsciously give other people permission to do the same. As we are liberated from our own fear, our presence automatically liberates others. Marianne Williamson (from Life is not an Accident, Jay Williams)

Love

Those who choose to love the parts of someone, even when they can't love the whole, often better both the parts and the whole.

Sometimes a walk alone can bring you together.

Love doesn't explain itself.
It's the question to which we have the perfect answer.

No sadness but death
so grips a loving parent,
as a shunning child.

You will never ride the horse itself,
for each of us has our own horse,
and this is the horse that someone you love
must ride,
the one that has appeared before her
and offered himself up for some difficult journey
—a crisis, a question, sometimes even a most troubling
answer—
that must be taken by her alone.

But if you are the friend she believes you to be,
you will have saddled her horse yourself,
held out your hands to lift her up,
wished her well,
let her know that your spirit will be with her
throughout her journey,
however long and difficult it may be,

and then—alone—
search out your own horse and mount it,
to meet her at every stop hers may make
along the way,
and encourage her, believe in her,
comfort her, *love* her,
and when her horse signals that she must board again,
repeat the process.

She will remember you wherever the horse takes her,
and look for you when he rests.

Colored memories
Rustling reds and oranges,
along with
yellows too—
Their beauty marks the end
of times that we
together knew.

The days when our tree
stood all alone,
when its green was just above,
when it provided us
with shade
and we, its green
our love.

Today, most green is gone,
though some is still
in view.
Enough, of course, to bring them back . . .
those memories
of you

REMEMBER

Remember?
Remember those times, our times,
the ones that we created,
the ones that belong to us,
the times that were that part of us
that made us shiver
with excitement
and joy
and anticipation,
the times that made us want all of
each other, badly, always,
and everywhere,
the times when we
left no time
for memories of mishaps, misdeeds
or mistakes,
the times when the words "I love you"
came naturally, and alone, without the need to
say out loud—or to ourselves—
"I mean it,"
in our effort to scale the walls
we have created with piled-on
unforgiving constructions of our past,
and true, actual, unhappy events
that we have adopted to live with us
for so long as we choose to "enjoy" their company,
or the times when
we could argue about one thing,
just one thing at a time,
to deal with that bruise,
the bruise of the moment,
without summoning up those legions of memories
poised to attack and destroy what we have

today
and the hopes we share
for tomorrow.

Remember?

I can't forget,
and I know that the strength of our best memories
will overcome our worst
and help us
one day at a time
to find our way back
to where we belong . . .
together
in love,
at peace with who we are,
understanding and not caring so much
who, at times,
we have been,
but loving who we can be,
who we must choose to be.

A poem after my father had walked into a hospital and the nurse
had mistaken him for my mother's father, not her husband,
because of the ravages of the disease that ultimately took his life.
He was an alcoholic, a gambler, a sinner, and a very good man.

My Dad

He wasn't my mother's father as the nurse had thought;

He was her husband,
but he was dying,

and I saw in his eyes that he understood
why the nurse had made her mistake.

So did we all.

He could have been anyone's father, however old—

Bent over, slouched, withered and wasted,
his last mirror had long ago called him old, and worse.

He deserved more than he had given himself, for though he was
weak in will,
his heart was strong, and good,
more admirable than reliable,
a better coach than a player,
knowing what should be done, wanting it done,
but having no idea
how to make the moves himself.

He was my father . . .
a drinker, a smoker, a collector of weaknesses,

but I will never forget his smile,
his warmth, his hugs and his humor,

or the razor-like rubbing of his stubble on my young face.

I only wish his last mirror would have reflected for him all of
this,
for though my memories of him conflict
they resolve—always —in favor
of the wonderful man he was.

FIRE AND ICE

I could see beyond all sunsets,
each morning by your side.
I could imagine no lands large enough
for you from me to hide
I could wait if you must wander
until you turn toward me,
yielding to my yearn.
Yet as the sunsets pass on through

and the morning bed is bare
the lands seem larger than I had dreamed,
too large for you to care.
You need not turn now. I understand.
For you the past was . . . nice.
For me, however, it was different . . .

say, as fire and ice.

No sand at any water's edge
however great or long,
no music played, no object made,
no morning Robin's song—

nothing, no one,
no place or thing,
nor any realm of any king,
rivals the thoughts I have of you
when, with our love,
we make one from two.

Believing in Tomorrow

History will come to us again,
as if, with our first touch,
it has stuck to us.

But for now,
(In these times, it is a good thing to say, "for now")
we say we have "grown apart,"
fallen from love,

as if history

would never revisit *us*,
(It is always *ours*, we tell ourselves,
 that hasn't the chance,)

as if all we ever were,
we would never be again,

as if all the reasons for all the smiles,
all the laughter,
were lost, never to be found again,

as if all the warm and love-filled nights,
those nights we dreamed on one pillow,
had melted away—

as if gold had taken on dust.

But gold it is (our history),
and it waits to be shined again—by us,
that it may one day gleam again.

This is what gold does.

History tells us so.

The Minute I heard My First Love Story, Rumi

The minute I heard my first love story
I started looking for you not knowing
how blind that was.
Lovers don't finally meet somewhere
They're in each other all along.

The best way to know life is to love many things. Vincent Van Gogh

---

Someday, after we have mastered the winds, the waves, the tides, and gravity, we shall harness for God the energies of Love. Then for the second time in the history of the world, man will have discovered fire.
Pierre Tielhard de Chardin

"the very thought of you
has my legs spread apart
like an easel with a canvas
begging for art"

— Rupi Kaur, Milk and Honey

W.H. Auden "As I walked out one evening"

I'll love you, dear, I'll love you
Till China and Africa meet,
And the river jumps over the mountain
And the salmon sing in the street.

I'll love you till the ocean
Is folded and hung up to dry
And the seven stars go squawking
Like geese about the sky.

He was my North, my South, my East and West,
My working week and Sunday rest.
My noon, my midnight, my talk, my song;
I thought that love would last forever: I was wrong.

W.H. Auden

I do not resemble your other lovers, my lady
should another give you a cloud
I give you rain
Should he give you a lantern, I
will give you the moon
Should he give you a branch
I will give you the trees
And if another gives you a ship
I shall give you the journey.   Nizar Qabbani

We come to love not by finding a perfect person, but by learning
to see an imperfect person perfectly. - Sam Keen, from To Love
and Be Loved

Love will fly if held too lightly
Love will die if held too tightly
Lightly, tightly, how do I know
Whether I'm holding or letting love go?

From Zen in the art of writing by Ray Bradbury, Oscar Wilde
poem

The best way to know life is to love many things. Vincent Van
Gogh

Someday, after we have mastered the winds, the waves, the tides, and gravity, we shall harness for God the energies of Love. Then for the second time in the history of the world, man will have discovered fire.
Pierre Tielhard de Chardin

Rodolph, Emma's first lover, thinks:

Emma was like all his other mistresses; and as the charm of novelty gradually slipped from her like a piece of her clothing, he saw revealed in all its nakedness the eternal monotony of passion, which always assumes the same forms and always speaks the same language. Madame Bovary, Gustave Flaubert

And Emma tried to imagine just what was meant, in life, by the words "bliss," "passion," and "rapture" - words that seemed so beautiful to her in books.

Love One Another

Love one another, but make not a bond of love.
Let it rather be a moving sea between the shores of your souls.
Fill each other's cup, but drink not from one cup.
Give one another of your bread, but eat not from the same loaf.
Sing and dance together and be joyous, but let each one of you be alone.
Even as the strings of a lute are alone though they quiver with the same music.
Give your hearts, but not into each other's keeping.
For only the hand of life can contain your hearts.
And stand together, yet not too near together.
For the pillars of the temple stand apart.
And the oak tree and the cypress grow not in each other's shadow.

Khalil Gibran

When, in disgrace with fortune and men's eyes,
I all alone betweep my outcast state,
And trouble deaf heaven with my bootless cries,
And look upon myself, and curse my fate,
Wishing me like to one more rich in hope,
Featured like him, like him with friends possessed,
Desiring this man's art and that man's scope,
With what I most enjoy contented least;
Yet in these thoughts myself almost despising,
Haply I think on thee—and then my state,
Like to the lark at break of day arising
From sullen earth, sings hymns at heaven's gate;
   For thy sweet love rememb'red such wealth brings
   That then I scorn to change my state with kings.
William Shakespeare

When he shall die
Take him and cut him out in little stars,
And he shall make the face of heaven so fine
That all the world will be in love with night
And pay no worship to the garish sun.

   Shakespeare, Romeo and Juliet

Warren and Mary discuss the hired man Silas who has returned
to their house, despite not being kin to them; Warren speaks first
and Mary answers:

"Home is the place where, when you have to go there,

They have to take you in."

" I should have called it
Something you somehow haven't to deserve."
The Death of the Hired Man, Robert Frost

Most people don't cheat because they're cheaters. They cheat because they're people. They are driven by hunger or for the experience of someone being hungry once more for them. They find themselves in friendships that take an unintended turn or they seek them out because they're horny or drunk or damaged from all the stuff they didn't get when they were kids. There is love. There is lust. There is opportunity. There is alcohol. And youth. And middle age. There is loneliness and boredom and sorrow and weakness and self-destruction and idiocy and arrogance and romance and ego and nostalgia and power and need. There is the compelling temptation of intimacies with someone other than the person with whom one is most intimate. Which is a complicated way of saying it's a long damn life. And people get mucked up in it from time to time. Even the people we marry. **Even us.**

Brave Enough, Cheryl Strayed

Separation
Your absence has gone through me
Like thread through a needle.
Everything I do is stitched with its color.

W.S. Merwin

"How lucky am I to have something that makes saying goodbye hard." – Winnie the Pooh

---

On our life together I want you to understand I shall not hold you to any medieval code of faithfulness to me nor shall I consider myself bound to you similarly . . . for I cannot guarantee to endure at all times the confinement of even an attractive cage.
Amelia Earhart from The Truth, Neil Strauss

The best way to know life is to love many things. Vincent Van Gogh

---

Someday, after we have mastered the winds, the waves, the tides, and gravity, we shall harness for God the energies of Love. Then for the second time in the history of the world, man will have discovered fire.
Pierre Tielhard de Chardin

You will learn a lot from yourself if you stretch in the direction of goodness, of bigness, of kindness, of forgiveness, of emotional bravery.

Be a warrior for love
                          Brave Enough, Cheryl Strayed

Fred Rogers always carried in his wallet a quote from a social worker that said, "Frankly, there isn't anyone you couldn't learn to love once you've heard their story."

"I wanted so badly to lie down next to her on the couch, to wrap my arms around her and sleep. Not fuck, like in those movies. Not even have sex. Just sleep together in the most innocent sense of the phrase. But I lacked the courage and she had a boyfriend and I was gawky and she was gorgeous and I was hopelessly boring and she was endlessly fascinating. So I walked back to my room and collapsed on the bottom bunk, thinking that if people were rain, I was drizzle and she was hurricane." — John Green, Looking for Alaska

———————————————————————————

"Do you know—I hardly remembered you?"
"Hardly remembered me?"
"I mean: how shall I explain? I—it's always so. Each time you happen to me all over again."
-Edith Wharton, The Age of Innocence

Parental Encouragement

Parents' words echo in the minds of their children long after the parents have gone. And they don't only echo, in the sense that the words are repeated. They come back to us in an exalted, weightier form, often with lessons and language our parents never dreamed of.

If they had only known, they would either have said more to us, more often, or held back the ammunition they simply did not know fit the self-destructive weapons we held in our minds.

Parental Encouragement: The right words, when directed at children, will resound for them throughout their lives. The parents' job is to find them.

I wrote this letter when my son Ryan made the Duke Basketball team, thinking of how difficult it is to compete daily against some of the best basketball players in the country. Both my sons, Justin and Ryan, earned positions on the team, and each of them worked hard every day to prove to themselves and others that they deserved that honor.

Dear Ryan,
On your way to the next practice, remember where you're going; remember where you've been; think of why you're going and think of why it's hard. How could you have dreamed that one day, now too many days, you would wake up knowing that you will drive to Cameron Indoor Stadium, walk into the same locker room with some of the best basketball players in the United States, your teammates, sit down and put on – as if it were some ordinary jersey – a Duke University Varsity Basketball jersey. And then, stand up, walk out onto the Cameron floor as a member of that legendary team. That's where you go, Ry, now nearly every day.

What's so special about that achievement, for a 6'3" kid from Shelburne Vermont? I think what's special about it is that you have given your best throughout your life; you started basketball late, but took it up with a vengeance. You struggled to catch your friends who were better than you, because they started before you, and you caught them, and passed them. You were never content with any part of your game. It would not come easy, you had reason to say, but it would come. That you believed, and you were right.

How many times did you not quit? How many hours have you spent working on your game? How many hours have you spent working on your body, to be stronger and quicker? How many times have you shaken your head in disappointment because your shot did not fall?

Could you have dreamed it would be as hard as it has been? I don't know about you, Ry, but I think this is the glory of who you are; you are determined to do what you can, and you do. Is it really fair for you to criticize yourself because some All-American basketball player is better than you? Do that, and you will never be happy, and you will have robbed yourself of all the joy that you have earned.

I hope, Ry, that you never look at practice as a time when you need to compete with All-Americans. That is not what practice should be for you. You are there for one purpose: to give whatever effort you can give. Some days that may be enough to compete with the best; some days it may not. You need to realize that whether your best is enough is wholly outside of your control. What is within your control is whether you give your best. As long as you do that, you should be proud.

Sure, it would be nice to say that as long as you work hard, do your best, you will be able to compete with the best college players in the US. But that may not be true. I want you to understand, though, that a person like you can influence the team in far more ways than the best of players. You are an inspiration to those gifted athletes who also work, and a conscience for those who don't.

I believe in you, and I know without a doubt that you could lose the ball 6 times in practice and have a greater positive impact on the team than if you had dunked 6 times. It's what you do after the mistakes that determines whether you and others benefit from them. If you curse yourself, drop your head, and demonstrate disgust, that is the reaction others will have.

Clearly, your mistakes don't call for smiles, but others should see that you are working to improve, that you care about the team, that you will do Ryan's best to contribute. And that the reason you are who you are is that you don't have the time to criticize yourself; you're too busy working to improve yourself.

If you show this attitude, Ry, however many mistakes you make, other, better players will see you coming nearer to them. They will know that Ryan may not be an All-American basketball player, but he is a player who will do what he can. And tomorrow, Ryan Caldbeck will be better than he was yesterday. That is the key to who you are Ry. You inspire me, and I know you inspire many others.

Don't play basketball if you need to be able to play at the same level every day as the Battiers and Carrawells. Play it because you have earned the right to be on the same floor with them, because you can play well enough to help the team, and because there is a lot more you can do for the team than play basketball. You can show them what it means to be a leader and a role model, and you can show them that the reason you work as hard as you do is not simply to improve your game; it's because that is more important than improving your game.

How good you get is never within your control. How much you

try, is. You have always done your best, Ry, and you should be so, so proud of that. Please don't let those difficult practices get you down. It must be so hard competing against such superb players every day without a break. Understand where you are Ry. The reason it is so hard, is that it is an incredible accomplishment. If it were easy, Ryan Caldbeck wouldn't be there.

Ry, it's OK to be disappointed when things happen you can't control. It isn't OK to be angry at yourself when things happen that you can't control. Reflect on the things in your life that you can control, and I think you will see that you have done exceptionally well. I can't imagine how hard it must be for you every day in practice. I only hope that you can "enjoy" it for the gift that it is. Someday, those turnovers will warm your heart as if each were a mountain that you had successfully climbed. Great things never come easily. And what you are doing is the greatest. I love you so much, Dad

---

I wrote this poem for my son Justin to let him know how incredibly proud he made me as a young man, and for the standards of excellence he set for his younger brother, Ryan.

To Justin, for the trails he has blazed, with love and admiration, Dad

  I remember
walking, with your hand in mine,
        I not thinking
    how soon
I would be the one
     missing the hand
       and *you*
    would be the one
extending yours.

I remember
the battles,
     the stretching and shaping of brothers' characters
in the driveway,
          not thinking how soon
 a younger brother's anger
would turn to admiration and love.

I remember the pride you took
in keeping the measure
     of talent
appropriately different
          between you and your brother,
as any older brother would want,
     not thinking how proud you would be
when the gap closed.

I remember your brother
looking up at you
          with distressed eyes
because you made him both proud
     and angry,
     not thinking that pride would outlast
anger.

And I remember
the lessons as they unfolded:
     the desire to excel, academic excellence,
          leadership, a love for basketball,
and—above all else—
          a passion for living,
     a love of friendship,
   and a community of friends,
     not thinking
of all
     that a parent could learn
from his child.

I remember the young man
      whose brother saw him
left alone
      on a college campus
afraid,
      but willing
         —and so able—
to begin to do what had to be done
to grow,
         not thinking of the enormity of the growth
     you had within you,
or the influence
your resolve would have
on your brother.

I remember the beginning,
how you knew enough
      to believe in yourself,
to put your hand out,
     to ask for the impossible,
to be given the answer of 'no',
        and to ignore it,
not thinking of the brother at home
     listening, paying attention, learning
        from trails you were forging,
discovering—through you—
his own abilities.

And I remember—ultimately—
my own feelings
    of growth
        as a father
with each goal you set,
each test you passed,
each friend you made,
each gift you shared,

     thinking

now

of the fullness you have given my life,

     of the pride I have in you,

of the lessons I have learned

and of the incomparable gifts

     you have bestowed

on one younger brother.

(I wrote this inscription on the inside cover of the book Basketball Joe, a great book on the values you learn from the game of basketball that apply to life just as well. I gave it to Ryan because it exemplified in its teachings the character, work ethic and attitude that Ryan had developed.)

Ry, This book (Basketball Joe, by Joseph J. Geiger) was written for you. It talks about dreams and goals, hard work and discipline, perseverance and character. It will show you that the path you have chosen on your own is the path to success and self-fulfillment.

Tomorrow night you will play in the Vermont High School Division 1 Semi-Finals. You have earned a starting position as a junior. You have made us—and Justin—so proud, not only for your accomplishments in basketball, but also for your hard work, your persistence, your efforts to do your best in all you do.

You are lucky, Ry. Tomorrow you will walk on to the court a winner, and you will leave as a winner—regardless of the score.

Believe in your abilities, Ry. Believe in yourself. You deserve to discover how good—and gifted—you are.

Love, Dad

Picasso: When he was a little boy, he said, "my mother told me if I decided to become a soldier I'd end up a general; if I decided to become a monk, I would end up a pope. I decided to become a painter, and ended up becoming Picasso."

I can't say that my mother made the point to me in the same way that Picasso's mother made it to him, but I do remember her telling me she loved me, that she was proud of me. And I remember feeling that I was special when I was in her company. That feeling stayed with me often enough so that I am thankful for having had the mother I did. She was closer for me to Picasso's mother, I'm sure, than I was for her, as a son, to Picasso.

Story told by the Dean of Harvard Business School, Kim B. Clark, at Graduation Ceremonies, 2003

When he was a young boy, his mother, he said, would never let him leave the house without taking him by the shoulders, looking him in the eyes, and saying, **"Remember who you are!"** Those words, he said, made him forever afraid to do anything that would embarrass the family, instead making him want to everything he could to make his friends and family proud. She was really saying, he realized, that he should remember that everything he did reflected not only on himself, but also on his father, and on his mother, his family, his grandparents, his friends, everyone who knew him and loved him. He was, she taught him, representing not only himself, but all those he loved as well.

His father, he told us, was a real cowboy, and the advice he most cherishes from his father was **"Always ride the high country."** Of course he meant that we should always do the right thing in life, but he meant more. So many people in life stay their comfort zones, unwilling to take risks; they don't explore. They don't ever leave the "valleys of their lives". Because of this, they never live the best lives they can live. It is only when we are willing to leave our comfort zones, to take risks to improve our lives, to expand our horizons, that we can see beyond those valleys and see all that life can give us.

A father handed his son a piece of smooth oak and said to him "this is your board. For every mistake you make, I will hammer in a nail." By the time the boy was thirteen, the board was covered corner to corner with nails, some rusted, some new. The father took the board to his son and said, "For every good thing that you do to fix all of these wrongs, I will take one nail out: It was not long before the father took the last nail out and proudly showed his son the clean piece of oak. "What about the holes?" the son asked. The father said, "The holes are what make the board beautiful." UNKNOWN

Our own "boards", if we really think of them in this way, make us appreciate not only "where we are" in life, but how far we've traveled to arrive.

Bless the parents who see the beauty in the holes of their child's board.

Excerpts from The Prophet

On Children

And a woman who held a babe against her bosom said, "Speak to us of Children."
And he said:
"Your children are not your children. They are the sons and daughters of Life's longing for itself. They come through you but not from you, And though they are with you, yet they belong not

to you. You may give them your love but not your thoughts. For
they have their own thoughts. You may house their bodies but
not their souls, For their souls dwell in the house of tomorrow,
which you cannot visit, not even in your dreams. You may strive
to be like them, but seek not to make them like you. For life goes
not backward nor tarries with yesterday. You are the bows from
which your children as living arrows are sent forth. The archer
sees the mark upon the path of the infinite, and He bends you
with His might that His arrows may go swift and far. Let your
bending in the archer's hand be for gladness; For even as he loves
the arrow that flies, so He loves also the bow that is stable."

When it comes to our children, we do not have the luxury of
despair. If we rise, they will rise with us every time, no matter
how many times we've fallen. Remembering that is the most
important work we can possibly do as parents. Cheryl Strayed

Parenting

A good parent is someone whose children may be average, but
they're always average in some very special way.

A young Snowy Egret

At first, I listened to the Eagles . . .
and I was sad.
Then I listened to my mother
who said, "No, your legs are not too long,
and your beak is just right," . . .
and, for the first time,
I was proud
to be
a Snowy Egret.

Parenting: Your child is gifted. Find the gifts, and nurture them.

Standing For Dreams

Someday
a child
will look at you
and ask, "how did you become . . . ?"
Make sure that child listens
to all that you have done.

Make sure he sees each dream of yours

as you fought along each day.
Make sure he knows of all the times
you stumbled on the way.

And teach him by each lonely fall
that dreams don't stoop for you;
the man who stops because he's down
won't see his dreams come true.

It's the man who rises from each fall.
It's the man who starts anew,
the man who's asked to give his best
and says, "that's what I do."
Tell him . . .
He will know you're right—
because that man
is you.

To Ryan with love and admiration
Dad, Christmas, 1998

(a gift he returned to me when he read this poem at the end of his
Senior Speech at the Duke University Basketball Banquet at
Cameron Indoor Stadium in 2001, the year they won the National
Championship, saying that he felt it applied to all of his
teammates as well.)

The following are words from a letter I wrote as a lawyer to
opposing lawyers and insurance adjusters in a case involving the
death of a child, in an effort to remind them—if only in a small
and imperfect way—of the joys children bring to their parents,
and the incomparable void left when they die.

*When you live in a small town, and your children live in that
same small town, and they have lived past those difficult teenage
years and worked themselves into young adults of whom you are*

proud, and they stop in to see you each day to ask how you're doing, or you stop by their home, and pet their dog, and have a beer, or no beer, and chat, and hug, and laugh, because they are unlike any other relationship you have, or could have, you carry that with you in your heart.

The memories warm you without notice. They will come when you are not with your children physically; they will come in the morning when you first wake up, or in the shower, or in the middle of a game you are watching, when you feel the need to call your child to let him know the game is on, or to joke, or just to let him know how much you love them.

And these memories never come alone. They come with pride, joy, and a fulfillment unlike anything else. And they come with a message of who you are, and who you want to be.

Our children make us better human beings. If we are role models, they are the reason we are. If they show us that they are weak, we understand our need to make them strong—and doing so makes them, and us, better. And when they show us that they are strong, their strength surges through us as if it were our own.

They are, as Sophocles taught us, the anchors of our lives.

And all of this is only a part of what our children mean to us.

It may be that without children our days can be filled in ways that make us content, but once children enter our lives they stretch our days, our lives, beyond what we could imagine. And if they leave us, if they die, those stretched days forever hang without shape as a constant reminder of all that is lost, and will never be.

A Mothers' Testimony

I am one mistake from great
if you don't add, don't remember,
and don't hold grudges.
I'm that close to great
only if my mother gets to testify
with no cross examination,
or my Golden Retriever (Jury was his name)
could speak on my behalf,
for he not only forgave, he forgot,
or if you could agree to read just that one quarter of my mind
that has made good decisions,
and presume the other seventy five percent innocent.
I'm just like I hope the rest of you are…
good enough to find comfort on my best days,
good enough to like most of who I am,
good enough to use the bad,
those weak parts of me,
to forgive others for their crimes,
and to hope, always, that one of their best days,
too,
is on its way
so we can celebrate
together
our mothers' testimony,
and continue our search
to make our mothers right.

The father called for his little boy.

The boy came and asked his father why he had called him.

"I just made this mirror, and I thought you might find it interesting," the father answered.

And so the little boy looked into the mirror.

"Daddy, all I see are pieces of me spread out all over!" Why is that?"

"That's because it's a truth mirror," the father said. "It shows you that there are really thousands of little pieces that make up who you are."

"But why are they all spread out the way they are?" the boy asked.

"Because it's our job every day to choose the pieces that we want to become."

Don't judge each day by the harvest you reap but by the seeds that you plant. Robert Louis Stevenson

---

A rich man asked a Zen master to write something down that would encourage the prosperity of his family for years to come, something joyful, something his family could cherish for generations. The master wrote, "Grandfather dies. Father dies. Child dies." The rich man became angry when he read what the Zen master had written. "I asked that you write something that would bring joy to our family! Why would you write something like this?" "What greater joy," the master replied, "can any of us ask, than that our children die last." Origin unknown

---

Nothing so affects the life of a child
as the unlived life of the parent. Carl Jung

When Gilda Radner, the Saturday Night Live comedian, was a child she always went to a busy beach with her parents. Everyone on the beach, it seemed to Gilda, used large identical umbrellas, making it very difficult for Gilda to find her parents whenever she'd leave for a swim or simply take a walk along the beach.

Because of this, she was terrified that she wouldn't be able to find her parents' umbrella. It was her greatest childhood fear. She told her dad that she was afraid, so her dad tied a pair of sneakers to their umbrella, making it easy for Gilda to find her parents. He told Gilda, "I don't want my little girl to be afraid." No longer was Gilda afraid.

Years later, when she was dying of cancer, and afraid, her husband, Gene Wilder, came to visit her in the hospital, carrying with him a miniature umbrella with sneakers tied to it.

No parent could ask for more from one small gesture than that his child years later may be comforted, again, as a result of his love.   Unknown

---

Bob Richards, the Olympic Gold medalist, wanted to play football in high school. He was skinny and smaller than many of his classmates. Still, he went to the try-outs. On the first day, he got knocked down repeatedly by the bigger and stronger boys. Each time, though, he kept at it, kept getting up, and kept doing whatever he could to make the team. Same thing second day. Same thing third day. When it came time to make the cuts, the coaches all felt that Bob Richards was too small to be a football player. "But what a heart he has," they all agreed. And just because he had never quit in try-outs, they put him on the team.

His first year, Bob Richards never missed a practice, never missed a game, and his father was in the stands every game cheering the team on. His son never played. Again, his sophomore year, he never missed a practice, never played in a game, but his father was in the stands for every game. By the time he was a senior he still had not played in a game, although he had never missed one, or missed a practice, and his father had attended every one of his games.

Then, during the season of his senior year, his father died. That weekend his team had a game. Bob Richards showed up. His coach said to him, "Bob, take some time off. We'll be OK." (Of course they'd be OK, they never played him anyway.) Bob replied, "No, Coach, I'd really like to suit up." So he did. And just like always, he sat on the bench.

Finally, at some point early in the second half, for the first time in his life, Bob Richards got up off the bench, walked up to his coach, and said, "Coach, will you please put me in this game?" The team was losing, but the game was not yet lost. The last thing the coach wanted to do was put Bob Richards in the game. But there he was, this boy who had worked his heart off for 4 years, never played, but never complained, and his father had just died. The coach couldn't say no.

Bob Richards played great. He scored two touchdowns. His team won the game.

Afterwards, in the locker room, as everyone was celebrating, Bob Richards went to his coach to thank him for letting him play. "I can't thank you enough for letting me play," he told his coach. " I knew that today was the first day ever that my dad could see me play, and I wanted to show him what I could do."

That father who had never missed a game throughout the 4 years that his son had never played, was *blind*. It had apparently never been important that he see his son play; he simply wanted to show his son that he loved him.

That is parenting.

This young man, who had the misfortune of being small and skinny when he decided he wanted to play football, had a parent who enabled him to ignore his weaknesses, to persevere past whatever barriers others could see, to believe in himself and, ultimately, to become an Olympic gold medalist.

His father may have been blind, but he could not have placed his gifts more precisely in the core of his son's heart.

Grief fills the room up of my absent child,
Lies in his bed, walks up and down with me,
Puts on his pretty looks, repeats his words,
Remembers me of all his gracious parts,
Stuffs out his vacant garments with his form. King John, III, iii, 93

[There is no fuller room than the empty familiar room of a child after that child has died; filled with his laughter and tears, his stories and fears, his promise gone, yet all somehow multiplied endlessly as we envision what might and should have been.]

"I believe that what we become depends on what our fathers teach us at odd moments, when they aren't trying to teach us. We are formed by little scraps of wisdom." Umberto Eco

---

"I'll tell you what my mom told me when I was 13. She says 'always get on the right bus with great people, and it'll take you to places that you can't get alone.' I've been at those two places, I'm still at one of them. The United States Military Academy and Duke are those two places." Coach Mike Krzyzewski

---

Parents teach their children how to be **warriors,** to give them the confidence to get on the horse to ride into battle when it's necessary to do so. If you didn't get that from your parents, **you have to teach yourself.**

Brave Enough, Cheryl Strayed

How worthless, how weak, how vanquished, how hollow it is to have a parent who exists but cannot reach, who says but will not be, who thinks but doesn't dare, who plays and plays and plays, but only, always, forever in the minor key. We sing the song of parenthood in only the major notes. Were you there? Did you love full-throttle? Did you fix it after you fucked it up?

Brave Enough, Cheryl Strayed

Make the Ordinary Come Alive
Do not ask your children
to strive for extraordinary lives.
Such striving may seem admirable,
but it is a way of foolishness.
Help them instead to find the wonder
and the marvel of an ordinary life.
Show them the joy of tasting
tomatoes, apples, and pears.
Show them how to cry
when pets and people die.
Show them the infinite pleasure
in the touch of a hand.
And make the ordinary come alive for them.
The extraordinary will take care of itself.

By William Martin, The Parent's Tao Te Ching: Ancient Advice for Modern Parents

---

A POEM FOR WOMEN WHO DON'T WANT CHILDREN

I won't preach about the rewards of motherhood.
I won't say it's the best thing that ever happened to me.
I won't say it's the best job I've ever had.
I won't say you'll regret not having a child.
I won't say you'll forget what life was like before.
I won't say it makes life worth living.
What I will say
is my son died.
What I will say
is I would still do it again.

Chanel Brenner

Do not let your children do anything that makes you dislike them.

Jordan B. Peterson, 12 Rules For Life, An Antidote to Chaos

"I never believed in Santa Claus. None of us kids did. Mom and Dad refused to let us. They couldn't afford expensive presents and they didn't want us to think we weren't as good as other kids who, on Christmas morning, found all sorts of fancy toys under the tree that were supposedly left by Santa Claus.
Dad had lost his job at the gypsum, and when Christmas came that year, we had no money at all. On Christmas Eve, Dad took each one of us kids out into the desert night one by one.
"Pick out your favorite star", Dad said.
"I like that one!" I said.
Dad grinned, "that's Venus", he said. He explained to me that planets glowed because reflected light was constant and stars

twinkled because their light pulsed.

"I like it anyway" I said.

"What the hell," Dad said. "It's Christmas. You can have a planet if you want."

And he gave me Venus.

Venus didn't have any moons or satellites or even a magnetic field, but it did have an atmosphere sort of similar to Earth's, except it was super hot-about 500 degrees or more. "So," Dad said, "when the sun starts to burn out and Earth turns cold, everyone might want to move to Venus to get warm. And they'll have to get permission from your descendants first.

We laughed about all the kids who believed in the Santa myth and got nothing for Christmas but a bunch of cheap plastic toys. "Years from now, when all the junk they got is broken and long forgotten," Dad said, "you'll still have your stars." – Jeannette Walls, The Glass Castle

---

"When a child first catches adults out—when it first walks into his grave little head that adults do not always have divine intelligence, that their judgments are not always wise, their thinking true, their sentences just—his world falls into panic desolation. The gods are fallen and all safety gone. And there is one sure thing about the fall of gods: they do not fall a little; they crash and shatter or sink deeply into green muck. It is a tedious job to build them up again; they never quite shine. And the child's world is never quite whole again. It is an aching kind of growing." – John Steinbeck, East of Eden

Perseverance

Remember, as you struggle, and as you grow,

that blossoms bloom at the branch's end.

It was a conversation they'd had so many times before . . .
(Success and Failure and Perseverance:)

"I'm tired," Failure said to Success, "I'll do it tomorrow".

"That's alright, I'll do it," said Success, turning to Perseverance.

 "Will you help me?"

Our Journeys

We name the greatest journeys of life
for their destination:
Ithaka, for example.
Marathon.
Nome (of Iditarod fame).

Each is *known* and *admired,* however, not as destinations,
but for the great journeys required to reach them.

We know Ithaka for its hardship, its daily distractions, its
heartache,
and for its relentless challenges that Odysseus

ultimately overcame.

His challenges are not unlike the distractions, excuses, procrastination,
victimhood, self-doubt, self-medication, rationalizations,
heartache—*Resistance*—
that keep the rest of us mired in mediocrity.

Marathon too. A simple city you will have made great
only if your journey to it started sufficiently far away.

And Nome. It's not the cold outside the warmed window that
makes Nome, Nome.
It's the teamwork—the 5 dogs that have never quit on you, or
you on them.
The eight days and nights. Long, long nights, with days that
offer no relief.
The ice, the slush, the snow, the loss of all your other dogs—
the ones you also loved.
The moose and the wolves.
The *aloneness* of it all.

These are the challenges that have given humble cities great
fame.
And it is in the journeys *to* them that Ithaka, and Marathon,
and Nome should be known.

Don't worry if the challenges in your life are not named after
the Ithaka of Odysseus, or the Marathon of Phiedippedes, or
the Nome of Rick Swenson.

Your challenges will come with different names.

Little, insignificant, unrecognized, names.

But they are *yours,* and they will come as small villages
along this river of life, their campfires burning in your eyes,
far enough from convenience that we choose to sail past
them,
or to simply make *no* choice, but to let the river flow.

Think of them as the shores of Forgiveness,
of Pride, or of Courage,
or Respect, Integrity and Persistence.

Smile when you reach shore,
not before.

Feel the *hardness* of it all.

The greatest journeys were made
that we might follow them,
and discover the greatness within our own.

What's important is not that you win, but that you *move.* We are
not losers because we lose, and we are not winners because we
win. It is our movement, our effort, our *progress*, that defines us.

When you find yourself wishing
that you could do better,
you're really wasting time—
It takes time to wish.

The way it is will become the way it was.
Hold on, and grow.

From time to time,
we should look back on our greatest failures
and give them the applause they deserve—
They, more than anything else, have helped us grow.

The best who are idle should fear the worst who are not.

The Birth
Tell me not the story of the hours spent,
Or the glory of one man's great ascent.

Show me its birth—his will to do Right—
For this is the lightening that lends him light.

A light not of power, but of control—
The cool will to set and pursue his goal.

With all the hours on his path to glory,
Will is the birth that begins his story.

Anyone who has coached understands the value of fundamentals.
He understands there is a right way and a wrong way to shoot a
basketball, throw a football or swing a golf club . . . and he will
do his best to teach the right way. But he can teach nothing more

critical to success—in sports or in life—than the value of perseverance.

The child who has learned the right way to shoot or throw or swing will never see success unless he forces himself to continue, to shoot more, to throw more, or swing more, than anyone else.

He needs to do it most when he doesn't want to do it at all. He needs to work his way through each failure that shows up after he's felt success. He needs to understand that what he hopes for he will never have, that all he has gained will be lost, that talent means nothing more than a product of very hard, and unpleasant, work. He ultimately needs to know that only if he is his fiercest competitor will he excel.

Finally, he should keep in mind that when he hears others question him, "Is it worth it?", he may well be on the right path.

Perseverance: It is a motion, however still it seems, because you are *moving through,* and will not be stopped. It is the difference-maker of life, and—always—the difference between who you are today and who you will become tomorrow.

There are two kinds of failure—one that comes at the *end,* and one that you make the beginning. The difference between them is you.

The way it is,
is to make us stronger.

Lost Opportunities

It is the remnants I want —
those parts of lessons we pick up momentarily
and admire
and then put down
in order to continue
along that wide and level path
of lesser lives
from where we see signs
in the distance
of our
own abandoned remnants
working for others,
others who chose to hold on to them,
to honor them,
and treat them with the respect
they earned
while away from us,
with others,
because *we chose*
to put them down.

I wrote this poem for my son Justin when he made the Duke basketball team, recognizing the challenges that an athlete faces who "walks on" to a team the caliber of Duke University's basketball team, and the contributions that such an athlete, with the proper focus, can make to the team.

The poem speaks to the role that "walk-ons" (those who make the team but don't receive a scholarship) play, giving all they can to make the "stars" better while realizing—and accepting—that their efforts will go unnoticed by most.

Tribute to a Walk-on

As Darkness lends its gift to night
putting the stars within our sight,
and mountains seem to scrape the skies
as valleys enhance their envied size,
one need not ever be the best
so long as he will never rest.
For as winds to wings, by his great gift,
himself, with others, he will lift.

I wrote this poem thinking of my mother, and really of all the
elderly whom we love and want "for them" to do more, to walk
more, to be more active, more involved, more healthy, more
alert, not thinking that she (or they) want the same.

Thoughts in a Chair

When flesh is old and tired and worn
and love is behind and pages are torn,
when children are gone and friends are away
and games are for closets, for others to play,

try as I might
— if I could then I would —
I am left with my guilt:
"If I could then I *should*."

I know that there's more
than my flesh and my pain
I know that the skies
have both sun and the rain.

I know I can do it,
or could at one time.

Begin. Open. *Anywhere.*

If others could wait . . .
this bell, it will chime.

But if there be sounds that never are heard,
our wishes unmatched by will,
my hope is that here—in the midst of my fear—
I can trust that you stand by me still.

If only we dreamed that our dreams
Must have their hard beginnings too,
We might then be better able
To make more of our dreams come true.

For a star to be born, there is one thing that must happen: a
gaseous nebula must collapse.
So collapse.
Crumble.
This is not your destruction.
This is your birth.
                    Annie Neugebauer

What counts in battle is what you do when the pain sits in. John
                    Short

Nothing in the world can take the place of persistence.
Talent will not; nothing is more common than unsuccessful men
with talent. Genius will not; unrewarded genius is almost a
proverb. Education alone will not; the world is full of educated
derelicts. Persistence and determination alone are omnipotent.
The slogan "press on" has solved and always will solve the

problems of the human race. Calvin Coolidge

It's a little like wrestling a gorilla. You don't quit when you're tired, you quit when the gorilla is tired. Robert Strauss

---

"On the plains of hesitation lay the blackened bones of countless millions who, at the dawn of victory, lay down to rest, and, resting, died." (Old saying)

From article in Sports Illustrated coffee table book

Stephen Dunn, a great poet and a lover of basketball, explaining the similarities between writing poetry and being guarded by a player who makes it difficult for you to excel.

"The equivalent in poetry writing would be not just to know, say, that Yeats is a great poet (obviously that's desirable), but to have the achievements of Yeats block your ability to write poetry every time you tried. The poets who keep writing do so in the face of such greatness. If they were reasonable, they'd stop. There's much to be said for obsessiveness and stubbornness. Poets need to be somewhat driven in order to push forward; talent isn't quite enough." Basketball and Poetry, Stephen Dunn

---

Case files of the Tracker, Tom Brown, Jr.

A man found a cocoon of a butterfly. One day a small opening appeared; he sat and watched the butterfly for several hours as it struggled to force its body through that little hole. Then it seemed to stop making any progress. It appeared as if it had gotten as far as it could and it could go no farther. Then the man decided to help the butterfly, so he took a pair of scissors and snipped off the remaining bit of the cocoon. The butterfly then emerged easily. But it had a swollen body and small, shriveled wings.

The man continued to watch the butterfly because he expected that, at any moment, the wings would enlarge and expand to be able to support the body, which would contract in time. Neither happened! In fact, the butterfly spent the rest of its life crawling around with a swollen body and shriveled wings. It never was able to fly.

What the man in his kindness and haste did not understand was that the restricting cocoon and the struggle required for the butterfly to get through the tiny opening were nature's way of forcing fluid from the body of the butterfly into its wings so that it would be ready for flight once it achieved its freedom from the cocoon.

Sometimes struggles are exactly what we need in our life. If nature allowed us to go through our life without any obstacles, it would cripple us. We would not be as strong as what we could have been. And we could never fly...

"It is impossible for you to go on as you were before, so you must go on as you never have."
Cheryl Strayed — Tiny Beautiful Things

The heights by great men reached and kept
Were not attained by sudden flight,
But they, while their companions slept,
Were toiling upward in the night.

Longfellow

Come, my friends,
Tis not too late to seek a newer world...
It may be that the gulfs will wash us down:
It may be we shall touch the Happy Isles,
And see the great Achilles, whom we knew.
Tho' much is taken, much abides; and tho'
We are not now that strength which in old days
Moved earth and heaven; that which we are, we are;
One equal temper of heroic hearts,
Made weak by time and fate, but strong in will
To Strive, to seek, to find, and not to yield.

From Alfred, Lord Tennyson's "Ulysses"

The Middle Eastern potentate called a meeting of the wise men in his kingdom, and he said, 'I want you to gather all the world's most significant knowledge together in one place so that my sons can read it and learn.' The wise men went off, and after a year, they came back with twenty-five volumes of knowledge.

 The potentate looked at it and he said, 'No, it's too long. Make it shorter.' So the wise men went off for another year and they came back with one single volume. The potentate looked at it and said, "No, still too long." So the wise men went off for another year and they came back and gave the potentate apiece of paper with one sentence on it.

A single sentence. You know what the sentence was? The sentence was " this too shall pass."

Know it all: One man's humble quest to become the smartest person in the world A. J. Jacobs

---

I hated every minute of training, but I said, "Don't quit. Suffer now and live the rest of your life as a champion."

Muhammad Ali

George Washington lost 2/3 of the major campaigns of the Revolutionary war; When Handel wrote The Messiah, he was at the lowest point in his life, sick, destitute and so in debt his creditors threatened debtor's prison; Louis Pasteur didn't discover pasteurization until he'd had a stroke; Henry Ford failed and went broke five times before he finally succeeded; His first Ford he forgot to put a reverse gear in it.; Albert Fuller was fired from three jobs and couldn't find work, so he started selling brushes door to door; Theodore Geisel wrote a children's book and submitted it to a publisher. The book was rejected by twenty three publishers. The twenty fourth bought it, published and sold six million copies. The book was "And to think that I saw it on Mulberry Street" (by Dr. Seuss); General Douglas MacArthur was turned down twice by West Point, only admitted on his third application; Tom Monahan's pizza business was failing in 1960, lost all in a fire in 1968, insurance reimbursed him ten cents on the dollar, he invested all in new shop, two years later bank repossessed, then ten months later gave it back to him, failing, he was $1.5 million dollars in debt, then he decided to deliver pizza, now called Domino's; on his 22nd try Richard Hooker finally convinced a publisher that war could be funny, with his book MASH; A record promoter asked Pat Williams if he would let a young singer sing during time outs, etc. at a 76er's game. Pat didn't like the idea but told the kid if he could convince the technicians it's ok with me, but why, he asked the kid would he want to sing at a basketball game, said he sings wherever he can so people will hear him, Williams said he got some applause after he sang, next few weeks heard him on the radio, singing same song, Mandy. The kid's name was Barry Manilow.

Go For the Magic, by Pat Williams

Ah, but a man's reach should exceed his grasp,
Or what's a heaven for?
— Robert Browning

Mother to Son, by Langston Hughes

Well, son, I'll tell you:
Life for me ain't been no crystal stair.
It's had tacks in it,
And splinters,
And boards torn up,
And places with no carpet on the floor –
Bare.
But all the time
I'se been a-climbin' on,
And reachin' landin's,
And turnin' corners,
And sometimes goin' in the dark
Where there ain't been no light.
So boy, don't you turn back.
Don't you set down on the steps
'Cause you finds it's kinder hard.
Don't you fall now --
For I'se still goin', honey,
I'se still climbin',
And life for me ain't been no crystal stair.

And though you cannot go back
And make a brand-new start, my friend.
Anyone can start from now
And make a brand-new end.

Author unknown, from The Difference Maker by John C. Maxwell

Those who do me wrong
whenever I remake a song
should know what issue is at stake
it is myself that I remake. Yeats

We confess before thee that if life were all smooth, there would be no patience; were it all easy, no courage, no sacrifice, no depth of character. We acknowledge before thee that what is most admirable is the child of adversity and of courageous souls unafraid to face it.

Harry Emerson Fosdick (Fred Rogers quoted this to friend Tim Madigan - from "I'm Proud of You".)

All that is gold does not glitter,
Not all those who wander are lost.
The old that is strong does not wither,
Deep roots are not reached by frost.

J.R.R. Tolkien "Lord of the Rings"

The greater danger for most of us is not that our aim is too high

and we miss it, but that it is too low and we reach it.
Michelangelo

My candle burns at both ends;
  It will not last the night;
But, ah, my foes, and oh, my friends -
  It gives a lovely light!

        First Fig
Edna St. Vincent Millay
"A Few Figs From Thistles"

We shall not flag nor fail. We shall go on to the end. We shall
fight in France and on the seas and oceans; we shall fight with
growing confidence and growing strength in the air.
We shall defend our island whatever the cost may be; we shall
fight on the beaches, landing grounds, in fields, in streets and on
the hills. We shall never surrender and even if, which I do not
for the moment believe, this island or a large part of it were
subjugated and starving, then our empire beyond the seas, armed
and guarded by the British Fleet, will carry on the struggle until
in God's good time the New World, with all its power and might,
sets forth to the liberation and rescue of the Old. (From the
speech of June 4, 1940)
AFTER DUNKIRK Winston Churchill

When you're going through hell, keep going. Winston Churchill

---

When things go wrong as they sometimes will;
When the road you're trudging seems all uphill;
When the funds are low, and the debts are high
And you want to smile, but have to sigh;
When care is pressing you down a bit-

Rest if you must, but do not quit.

Success is failure turned inside out;
The silver tint of the clouds of doubt;
And you can never tell how close you are
It may be near when it seems so far;
So stick to the fight when you're hardest hit-
It's when things go wrong that you must not quit.

"Don't Quit," Author Unknown

Success seems to be largely a matter of hanging on after others
have let go. William Feather

Somebody said it couldn't be done,
But he with a chuckle replied
That "maybe it couldn't," but he would be one
Who wouldn't say so until he had tried.
So he buckled right in with a trace of a grin
On his face. If he worried he hid it.
He started to sing as he tackled the thing
 that couldn't be done, and he did it.

Somebody scoffed: "Oh, you'll never do that;
At least no one ever has done it'"
 But he took off his coat and he took off his hat,
And thee first thing we knew he'd begun it.
With a lift of his chin and a bit of a grin,
Without any doubting or quiddit,
He started to sing as he tackled the thing
That couldn't be done, and he did it.

There are thousands to tell you it cannot be done,
There are thousands to prophesy failure;
There are thousands to point out to you one by one,

The dangers that wait to assail you.
But just buckle in with a bit of a grin,
Just take off your coat and go to it'
Just start to sing as you tackle the thing
That "cannot be done, " and you'll do it.

It couldn't be done Edgar A,. Guest

God provides the wind, but man must raise the sails. St.
Augustine

There's no greater foolishness in the world than for a man to
despair …. Great hearts, my dear master, should be as patient in
adversity as they are joyful in prosperity.
Don Quixote, by Miguel De Cervantes

Out of the night that covers me,
Black as the Pit from pole to pole,
I thank whatever gods may be
For my unconquerable soul.
     Invictus, by William Ernest Henley

In the fell clutch of circumstance
I have not winced nor cried aloud.
Under the bludgeonings of chance
My head is bloody, but unbowed.

Beyond this place of wrath and tears
Looms but the horror of the shade,
And yet the menace of the years
Finds, and shall find me, unafraid.

It matters not how strait the gate,
How charged with punishments the scroll,
I am the master of my fate;
I am the captain of my soul.
                    Invictus, by William Ernest Henley

Anne Lamott, Bird by Bird (told to students who often feel
overwhelmed when they focus on the size of their projects)

. . . my older brother, who was ten years old at the time, was
trying to get a report on birds written that he'd had three months
to write, which was due the next day. We were out at our family
cabin in Bolinas, and he was at the kitchen table close to tears,
surrounded by binder paper and pencils and unopened books on
birds, immobilized by the hugeness of the task ahead. Then my
father sat down beside him, put his arm around my brother's
shoulder, and said, "Bird by bird, buddy. Just take it bird by
bird."

If you're going to try, go all the way. Otherwise, don't even start.
This could mean losing girlfriends, wives, relatives and maybe
even your mind. It could mean not eating for three or four days.
It could mean freezing on a park bench. It could mean jail. It
could mean derision. It could mean mockery – isolation.
Isolation is the gift. All the others are a test of your endurance, of
how much you really want to do it. And, you'll do it, despite
rejection and the worst odds. And it will be better than anything
else you can imagine. If you're going to try, go all the way. There
is no other feeling like that. You will be alone with the gods, and

the nights will flame with fire. You will ride life straight to perfect laughter. It's the only good fight there is. – Charles Bukowski

---

The committee judged the promises and offers of this mission to be impossible, vain, and worthy of rejection: that (it) was not proper to favor an affair that rested on such weak foundations and which appeared uncertain and impossible...
- Talavera Commission, 1491, turning down Christopher Columbus' proposal for finding a new trade route to the Indies. Queen Isabella of Spain later funded the project.

"Success is going from failure to failure without a loss of enthusiasm."
~Sir Winston Churchill

The benefits of struggling—of being challenged, afraid, pained, confused—are so precious that if they could be bottled, people would pay dearly for them.
But they can't be bottled. And if you want the wisdom, the strength, the clarity, the courage that can come from struggle, the price is clear: you have to endure the struggle first.

Eric Greitens, Resilience, hard-won wisdom for living a better life

---

More dangerous than the worst is the pretty good you can no longer tell from the best. James Richardson

---

We don't rise to the level of our expectations. We fall to the level of our training. Archilochus

---

"A black belt is just a white belt who never quit."
The Brain Warrior's Way, Daniel Amen, Tana Amen

"When that this body did contain a spirit, a kingdom for it was too small a bound."
Henry IV, Part one, Act 5, Scene 4 (favorite quote from prisoner serving life sentence, after 10 years of solitary confinement in "Shakespeare Saved My Life", by Laura Bates)

Failure is not a destination.
Don't stop where you fail.

Coach Mike
Krzyzewski

Nobody will protect you from your suffering. You can't cry it away or eat it away or starve it away or punch it away or even therapy it away. It's just there, and you have to survive it. You have to endure it. You have to live through it and love it and move on and be better for it and run as far as you can in the direction of your best and happiest dreams across the bridge that was built by your own desire to heal. Therapists and friends can help you along he way, but the healing—the genuine healing, the actual real-deal, down-on-your-knees-in-the-mud change—is entirely and absolutely **up to you.**
Brave Enough, Cheryl Strayed

Of all the virtues we can learn, no trait is more useful, more essential for survival, and more likely to improve the quality of life than the ability to transform adversity into an enjoyable challenge. Mihaly Csikszentmihalyi

---

Every last one of us can do better than give up.
                              Brave Enough, Cheryl Strayed

The benefits of struggling—of being challenged, afraid, pained, confused—are so precious that if they could be bottled, people would pay dearly for them.

But they can't be bottled. And if you want the wisdom, the strength, the clarity, the courage that can come from struggle, the price is clear: you have to endure the struggle first.

Eric Greitens, Resilience, Hard-won Wisdom for Living a Better Life

---

Who has no chaos inside him will never give birth to a dancing star.

                    Thus Spoke Zarathustra, Nietzsche

Art takes time. Monet grew his gardens before he painted them.
Book or poetry, "Love Her Wild" by Atticus

It is only by drawing often, drawing everything, drawing incessantly, that one fine day you will discover to your surprise that you have rendered something in its true character.
Camille Pissarro

They tried to bury us. They didn't know we were seeds.
Dinos Chrisitanopoulos, poet

---

the most beautiful thing in this world isn't made
up of particles. it's the strength of the person who
has seen the collapse of their world , everything
they held dear crashing down in a million pieces.
yet every morning they wake up and build their
life, all over again, mourning their loss in a
tranquil silence. I haven't yet seen
anything more astonishingly beautiful.

yesterday I was the moon by noor unnahar

If you're going to try, go all the way. Otherwise, don't even start. This could mean losing girlfriends, wives, relatives and maybe even your mind. It could mean not eating for three or four days. It could mean freezing on a park bench. It could mean jail. It could mean derision. It could mean mockery–isolation. Isolation is the gift. All the others are a test of your endurance, of how much you really want to do it. And, you'll do it, despite rejection and the worst odds. And it will be better than anything else you can imagine. If you're going to try, go all the way. There is no other feeling like that. You will be alone with the gods, and the nights will flame with fire. You will ride life straight to perfect laughter. It's the only good fight there is. — Charles Bukowski, Factotum

Reading

Every day of your life you have an opportunity to sit down with someone who will educate you in whatever way you wish, someone who will make you laugh—and make you funnier yourself—, someone who will make you cry in a way that makes you more grateful for the life you have, someone who will help you overcome the obstacles in your life by showing you how he overcame similar obstacles in his life, someone who expresses your feelings in ways that help you better understand who you are, someone who will show you what it takes to become a hero, a failure, a sinner or a saint; you will have the opportunity to discover, and all you need to do … is *read*.

Reading: A path to destinations we had not known existed, and to others that we will create.

Always keep a good book within reach. Almost certainly it wants to tell you something that will help you.

Read, but experience. The goal is to experience as much of life as you can. Do things; be as active as you can be. What you see others do, force yourself to try it if it interests you. Don't let others satisfy your need for growth by their own. Teach if you care to teach; play when you're in the mood; travel, experience things that will help you grow, change professions if yours is not fulfilling you.

And books? They will help teach you throughout life, help you learn what activities or interests you should pursue next. They show you others' mistakes and accomplishments. They are the grist of life in that they must be worked and ground to their essence. Once done, we can take what they have to offer and try their lessons in our own lives.

The man who does not read good books has no advantage over the man who cannot read them. Mark Twain

---

Tom Sawyer on doing everything by the book:

"Don't I tell you it's in the books? Do you want to go to doing different from what's in the books, and get things all muddled up?" The Adventures of Huckleberry Finn, Mark Twain

---

He ate and drank the precious
        Words,
His spirit grew robust;
He knew no more that he was
        Poor,
Nor that his frame was dust.
He danced along the dingy
        Days,
And this bequest of wings
Was but a book. What liberty
A loosened spirit brings! Emily Dickinson

"So today, whether you woke up feeling defeated or unstoppable, know there is a sentence hidden away on a library shelf somewhere that understands exactly how you feel." Andrea Diamond

---

Imaginary gardens with real toads in them. ~Marianne Moore's definition of poetry, "Poetry," Collected Poems, 1951

So he who would lead a Christ-like life is he who is perfectly and absolutely himself. He may be a great poet, or a great man of science; or a young student at a University, or one who watches sheep upon a moor; or a maker of dramas, like Shakespeare, or a thinker about God, like Spinoza; or a child who plays in a garden, or a fisherman who throws his nets into the sea.

It does not matter what he is, as long as he realizes the perfection of the soul that is within him. All imitation in morals and in life is wrong. Through the streets of Jerusalem at the present day crawls one who is mad and carries a wooden cross on his shoulders. He is a symbol of the lives that are marred by imitation.

Father Damien was Christ-like when he went out to live with the lepers, because in such service he realized fully what was best in him. But he was not more Christ-like than Wagner, when he realized his soul in music; or than Shelley when he realized his soul in song.

There is no one type for man. There are as many perfections as there are imperfect men. Such perfections are the aim of literary education, and if perfection is rarely the actual result, the process is no less noble for that.

Why Read? By Mark Edmundson, Excellent book on reading to improve our lives.

To the true reader, every form of usable truth is usable many times over. Later in life Emerson is more circumspect: "Shall I tell you the secret of the true scholar? It is this: Every man I meet is my master in some point, and in that I learn of him." Why Read? By Mark Edmundson

---

Ink runs from the corners of my mouth.
There is no happiness like mine.
I have been eating poetry.

Mark Strand (From "Best Loves")

. . . Good. Now here's what poetry can do.
Imagine yourself a caterpillar.
There's an awful shrug and, suddenly,
You're beautiful for as long as you live.
     Poet: Stephen Dunn
Poem: "Poem For People That Are Understandably Too Busy To Read Poetry"

It is difficult
to get the news from poems
yet men die miserably every day
for lack
of what is found there.

William Carlos Williams

When power leads man toward arrogance, poetry reminds him of his limitations. When power narrows the areas of man's concern, poetry reminds him of the richness and diversity of his existence. When power corrupts, poetry cleanses, for art establishes the basic human truths which must serve as the touchstone of our judgment.
- - - John F. Kennedy- Address, Amherst College, October 26, 1963

To educate for the future, one must educate for the moment. Classes should sprawl beyond particular subjects. In digressions lie lessons. Expose students to possibilities. Let them know your fondness for china, birds, tag sales and gardening. Talk to them about economics and sociology, to be sure, but also about places you have been and things you have seen and thought. Instill the awareness that for the interested person days and nights glitter.

Samuel Pickering (the model for the English Teacher in the film Dead Poets Society.) Book by Book by Michael Dirda

---

Neil Gaiman illustrates . . . with the most breath-stopping testament to what we endure for stories as they in turn help us endure, by way of his 97-year-old cousin Helen, a Polish Holocaust survivor:
A few years ago, she started telling me this story of how, in the ghetto, they were not allowed books. If you had a book … the Nazis could put a gun to your head and pull the trigger — books were forbidden. And she used to teach under the pretense of having a sewing class… a class of about twenty little girls, and they would come in for about an hour a day, and she would teach them maths, she'd teach them Polish, she'd teach them grammar…
One day, somebody slipped her a Polish translation of Margaret Mitchell's novel Gone with the Wind. And Helen stayed up — she blacked out her window so she could stay up an extra hour, she read a chapter of Gone with the Wind. And when the girls came in the next day, instead of teaching them, she told them what happened in the book.
And each night, she'd stay up; and each day, she'd tell them the story.
And I said, "Why? Why would you risk death — for a story?" And she said, "Because for an hour every day, those girls weren't in the ghetto — they were in the American South; they were

having adventures; they got away.

I think four out of those twenty girls survived the war. And she told me how, when she was an old woman, she found one of them, who was also an old woman. And they got together and called each other by names from Gone with the Wind...

We [writers] decry too easily what we do, as being kind of trivial — the creation of stories as being a trivial thing. But the magic of escapist fiction ... is that it can actually offer you a genuine escape from a bad place and, in the process of escaping, it can furnish you with armor, with knowledge, with weapons, with tools you can take back into your life to help make it better... It's a real escape — and when you come back, you come back better-armed than when you left.

Helen's story is a true story, and this is what we learn from it — that stories are worth risking your life for; they're worth dying for. Written stories and oral stories both offer escape — escape from somewhere, escape to somewhere.

"One must be careful of books, and what is inside them, for words have the power to change us."

—Cassandra Clare, *The Infernal Devices*

Self-Reliance

When in times of great need
there is a knock on the door of your soul,
you are the one who must answer it.

You can dream up all your wishes
your wants and lists to do.

You can wait, as if tomorrow
will bring you something new.

No days, however, no reverie,
no hope that change is due,

can better the life you live today
without an act from you.

Once upon a time
a child was given a magic ring,
and was told it could only be used once.
Because of this, the child persevered on her own, through all
the struggles of her life—
She wanted to save the ring's magic
for when she might really need it,
for that time she knew would someday come.

She never needed it.

"Look For Yourself"

The Story

It was their last day. The two students were saying goodbye to their Zen Master, and as they began their life's journey he said to them, "Remember—Always look for your self."

And with that last advice, they parted ways.

Many years later, the two students came across each other, and they were curious to see how each other's lives had evolved.

"I have not led a good life," the first student said.

"I have done just what our master instructed—I have looked out for myself in all parts of my life; I've looked to others for what they might do for me, and cared nothing for what I might do for them; I've helped myself to more and more, before others even had enough; I've lived my life looking out for no one but myself, and our master could not have been more wrong—none of this has fulfilled me.

"But the master didn't actually say, 'Look *out* for yourself,'" the second student replied.

"He said, 'Look for your self,' and there is a difference."

"I have looked for my self throughout my life," the second student explained.

"I've looked for my self in those who are weak, so that I might better understand their weaknesses, and my own, for I have weaknesses myself.

"I have looked for my self in everyone who has hurt me, for I have hurt others myself, and wish I had not.

"I've looked for my self in those whom I have forgiven and in those who have forgiven me, for we are the same, and forgiveness has given us a peace, and made each of us better.

"I've looked for my self also in those who are better than I am, those who are stronger than I am, and those who are wiser than I am, for in their goodness, in their strength and in their wisdom, I see what I can be.

"Yes, I have looked for my self in every wrong that others commit against me, with the hope that I will understand those who do me wrong—and myself—better.

"And I have looked for my self in every good that others do, with the hope that I might do such good myself.

"Our Master was right—*Look for your self.*

Your lessons are in the search."

Adapted from a similar story in the epilogue in *All Things Shining*, by Hubert Dreyfus and Sean Dorrance Kelly

IMAGINE

Imagine
if you listened
        to all your deepest thoughts

the ones that let you wander,
                through self-created plots.

Imagine choosing differently,
      for you and not for them,
of whom you might discover
           of whom you might have been.

Imagine, 'magine, 'magine
              the freeness of it all,
of choices lust,
not choices must,
      no father-fights, no pall.

Imagine once
  to let you loose,
      to live your life of lust,
         imagine just to run the race
without the words "you must."

Or,

imagine rules that show the light
of lessons learned before,
of what it means to have a guide,
a sail to reach the shore.

Imagine it all, free and fixed,
and look to which is best

our choice, our chance,
are reasons
why
our life, or not, is blessed.

So let the music play on
and on,
let the tempo slow,
let the singers source their songs,
let the trumpets blow,

but let your heart still dance its will—
the sounds may serve as guide,
but the beat that must be borne
is the beat you bear inside.

Be true to yourself. God has worked years to put together a package unlike any other he has created. You have a unique combination of gifts. You need to explore your gifts, and understand that you have them for a reason.

There will be many opportunities for you to follow others' footsteps. You must remember that they were not you.

Their footsteps will either bore or frustrate you; they will go too far or not far enough.

Find your talents, and do what comes naturally for you. Your teachers are messengers only. They are neither better, nor worse, only different.

Limit yourself to what they have taught you and you have wasted the uniqueness you have to offer to the world.

You are the valley
that looks up to the mountains
in wonder,
yet you are as much the wonder as they—

for it is the valley that is the trees of the forests,
It is the valley that is the grass of the plains,
the crops and the cattle,
the farmer and the farm,
pastures, rivers and streams,
and it is the valley—you—
That nourishes us all
As we gaze at the mountains.

Give the mountains in your life their credit,
but remember, too, who you are.

[N]either believe nor reject anything because any other person, or description of persons rejected or believed it. Your own reason is the only oracle given you by Heaven . . . . Thomas Jefferson, from Excuses Begone by Dr. Wayne Dyer

---

No one, in my opinion, has better expressed the importance of self-reliance than Emerson. However much we learn from others, however much we emulate people in our lives, or even those with whom we've never had contact, however much we strive to become more like others, we are different, and it is that difference that we need to discover and hone. Anyone who doubts this needs only to read Emerson's words:

Insist on yourself; never imitate. Your own gift you can present every moment with the cumulative force of a whole life's cultivation; but of the adopted talent of another you have only an extemporaneous half possession. That which each can do best, none but his Maker can teach him. No man yet knows what it is, nor can, till that person has exhibited it.

Where is the master who could have taught Shakspeare? Where is the master who could have instructed Franklin, or Washington, or Bacon, or Newton? Every great man is a unique. The Scipionism of Scipio is precisely that part he could not borrow. Shakspeare will never be made by the study of Shakspeare.

Do that which is assigned you, and you cannot hope too much or dare too much. There is at this moment for you an utterance brave and grand as that of the colossal chisel of Phidias, or trowel of the Egyptians, or the pen of Moses or Dante, but different from all these.

Not possibly will the soul, all rich, all eloquent, with thousand-cloven tongue, deign to repeat itself; but if you can hear what these patriarchs say, surely you can reply to them in the same pitch of voice; for the ear and the tongue are two organs of one nature. Abide in the simple and noble regions of thy life, obey thy heart and thou shalt reproduce the Foreworld again. Emerson, Essay on Self-Reliance

---

Do not follow where the path may lead. Go instead where there is no path and leave a trail. Emerson

---

What lies behind us and what lies before us are tiny matters compared to what lies within us. Emerson

---

(Quietly) I neither could nor would rule my King. (Pleasantly) But there's a little..., area...where I must rule myself. It's very little - less to him than a tennis court.

(Thomas More agreeing to allow King Henry to rule him except in matters of his conscience.) A Man For All Seasons, Robert

Bolt

A bird doesn't sing because it has an answer, it sings because it has a song.
Maya Angelou

Today you are you! That is truer than true!
There is no one alive who is you-er than you.

Dr. Seuss

Strength of numbers is the
delight of the timid.
The Valiant in spirit glory in
fighting alone.
MOHANDAS KARAMCHAND GANDHI

If a man does not keep pace with his companions,
perhaps it is because he hears a different drummer.
Let him step to music which he hears however measured or far
away.   Henry David Thoreau

Do not believe in what you have heard;
do not believe in the traditions because they have been handed
down for generations;
do not believe in anything because it is rumoured or spoken by
many;
do not believe merely because a written statement of some old
sage is produced;
do not believe in conjectures; do not believe in that as truth to

which you have become attached by habit;
do not believe because of the authority of your teachers and
elders.
After observation and analysis, when it agrees with reason and is
conducive to the good and gain of one and all, then accept it,
practice it and live up to it.

Buddha

Our deepest fear is not that we are inadequate. Our deepest fear
is that we are powerful beyond measure. It is our light, not our
darkness that most frightens us. We ask ourselves, "Who am I to
be brilliant, gorgeous, talented, fabulous?" Actually, who are you
not to be? You are a child of God. Your playing small does not
serve the world. There is nothing enlightened about shrinking so
that other people won't feel insecure around you.

We are all meant to shine, as children do. We were born to make
manifest the glory of God that is within us. It's not just in some
of us; it's in everyone. And as we let our own light shine, we
unconsciously give other people permission to do the same. As
we are liberated from our own fear, our presence automatically
liberates others.

— Marianne Williamson (A Return to Love: Reflections on the
Principles of a Course in Miracles)

Trust Thyself: every heart vibrates to that iron string....Who so
would be a man, must be a nonconformist. He who would gather
immortal palms must not be hindered by the name of goodness,
but explore if it be goodness....   Emerson

Misunderstood! It is a right fool's word. Is it so bad then to be
misunderstood? Pythagoras was misunderstood, and Socrates and
Jesus and Luther, and Copernicus and Galileo and Newton and

every pure and wise spirit that ever took flesh. To be great is to be misunderstood. Emerson

---

What I must do is all that concerns me, not what the people think. This rule, equally arduous in actual. and in intellectual life, may serve for the whole distinction between greatness and meanness. It is the harder because you will always find those who think they know what is your duty better than you know it. It is easy in the world to live after the world's opinion; it is easy in solitude to live after our own; but the great man is he who in the midst of the crowd keeps with perfect sweetness the independence of solitude. Emerson

---

The Duke of Norfolk: Oh confound all this. I'm not a scholar, I don't know whether the marriage was lawful or not but dammit, Thomas, look at these names! Why can't you do as I did and come with us, for fellowship!
Sir Thomas More: And when we die, and you are sent to heaven for doing your conscience, and I am sent to hell for not doing mine, will you come with me, for fellowship?

….And when the last law was down, and the Devil turned round on you – where would you hide, Roper, the laws all being flat? (He leaves him) This country's planted thick with laws from coast to coast – man's laws, not God's – and if you cut them down – and you're just the man to do it – d'you really think you could stand upright in the winds that would blow then?

In response to Roper's accusing More of respecting God's law more than man's.
A Man For All Seasons, by Robert Bolt

Our remedies oft in ourselves do lie

Which we ascribe to heaven.

All's Well That Ends Well 1.i.199-200

Helena resolves to take the matters into her own hands to win the right to marry Bertram (proclaiming that she, rather than God, bears the responsibility for fixing her unhappiness)

On Consistency Ralph Waldo Emerson
A foolish consistency is the hobgoblin of little minds, adored by little statesmen and philosophers and divines. With consistency a great soul has simply nothing to do. He may as well concern himself with his shadow on the wall. Out upon your guarded lips! Sew them up with pack thread, do. Else, if you would be a man, speak what you think today in words as hard as cannon balls, and tomorrow speak what tomorrow thinks in hard words again, though it contradict everything you said today.... Fear never but what you shall be consistent in whatever variety of actions, so they be each hones and natural in their hour. For of one will, the actions will be harmonious, however unlike they seem. These varieties are lost sight of when seen at a little distance, at a little height of thought. One tendency unites them all. The voyage of the best ship is a zigzag line of a hundred tacks. This is only a microscopic criticism. See the line from a sufficient distance, and it straightens itself to the average tendency, your genuine action will explain itself and will explain your other genuine actions., (From the essay, Self-Reliance)
The inner Gleam Ralph Waldo Emerson

I READ the other day some verses written by an eminent painter which were original and not conventional. The soul always hears an admonition in such lines, let the subject be what it may. The sentiment they instill is of more value than any thought they may contain. To believe your own thought, to believe that what is true for you in your private heart is true for all men,--that is genius. Speak your latent conviction, and it shall be the universal sense; for the inmost in due time becomes the outmost, and our first thought is rendered back to us by the trumpets of the Last Judgment. Familiar as the voice of the mind is to each, the highest merit we ascribe to Moses, Plato and Milton is that they set at naught books and traditions, and spoke not what men, but what they thought. A man should learn to detect and watch that gleam of light which flashes across his mind from within, more than the lustre of the firmament of bards and sages. Yet he dismisses without notice his thought, because it is his. In every work of genius we recognize our own rejected thoughts; they come back to us with a certain alienated majesty. Great works of art have no more affecting lesson for us than this. They teach us to abide by our spontaneous impression with good-humored inflexibility then most when the whole cry of voices is on the other side. Else to-morrow a stranger will say with masterly good sense precisely what we have thought and felt all the time, and we shall be forced to take with shame our own opinion from another.

Emerson, Essay on Self-Reliance

If a man does not keep pace with his companions, perhaps it is because he hears a different drummer. Let him keep step to that music which he hears, no matter how measured or far away. Thoreau

---

In the end, it is important to remember that we cannot become what we need to be by remaining what we are. Max De Pree

---

This above all: To thine own self be true,
And it must follow, as the night the day,
Thou canst not then be false to any man.

William Shakespeare, Hamlet

Be who you are and say what you feel, because those who mind don't matter, and those who matter don't mind.

— Dr. Seuss

Our doubts are traitors, and make us lose the good we oft might win by fearing to attempt.

Shakespeare

"It seems to me," said Sancho, "that the knights who did all these things were driven to them...but...why should you go crazy? What lady has rejected you ...?"

"That is exactly it,", replied Don Quixote, "that's just how beautifully I've worked it all out – because for a knight errant to go crazy for good reason, how much is that worth? My idea is to become a lunatic for no reason at all ..." Cervantes, Don Quixote

---

Tell them that you know that your shoes are broken and that there are pimples on your face, yes, and that you have buck teeth and a club foot, but that you don't care, for tomorrow they are playing Beethoven's last quartets in Carnegie Hall and at home you have Shakespeare's plays in one volume. Nathaniel West, Miss Lonelyhearts

---

Aldous Huxley and other writers tried to convince Ray Bradbury that he should take Mescaline (a drug that can affect the mind) because they wanted him to tune in, turn on, and drop out, dangling before him the prospect of marvelous and abundant perceptions. He declined, telling the psychedelically inclined trio" "I don't want to have a lot of perceptions. I want to have one at a time. When I write a short story, I open the trapdoor on the top of my head, take out one lizard, shut the trapdoor, skin the lizard, and pin it up on the wall." From Chris Buckley's "But Enough About You"

Our deepest fear is not that we are inadequate. Our deepest fear is that we are powerful beyond measure. It is our light, not our darkness that most frightens us. We ask ourselves "Who am I to be brilliant, gorgeous, talented, fabulous?" Actually, who are you *not* to be? You are a child of God. Your playing small does not serve the world. There is nothing enlightened about shrinking so that other people won't feel insecure around you. We are all meant to shine, as children do. We were born to make manifest the glory of God that is within us. It'/s not just in some of us; it's in everyone. And as we let our own light shine, we unconsciously give other people permission to do the same. As we are liberated from our own fear, our presence automatically liberates others. Marianne Williamson (from *Life is not an Accident,* Jay Williams)

Appendix

A letter I wrote to my sons when they were about to leave home for college.

Dear Justin and Ryan,

Time has passed too quickly. I had wanted to teach my sons so much. And I had hoped that my lessons would come not as much from what I said as from what I did. I know that I have not shown you as I should have. It's because of this, as each of you gets closer to entering upon your own life's journey, that I thought it might be of help to write down some thoughts. Some of them may help you more than others. And, of course, you will learn your own lessons as you grow.

You will see lessons here that I have failed to keep myself. There is a point to be learned even from this: you can learn as much from another person's failures as from your own. And, what is more, you have your own abilities, unique to yourself, and you should always remember that no one else's failures should predict your own path.

Just as true, is that no one else's successes should lessen your own achievements. Never compare your own achievements with others'. You have no control over others' successes or failures. Pay attention only to your own gifts and strive, always, only to do the best with what you have. In some cases it will place you first; in others it will place you last. But in all cases it will fill your spirits and provide you with a contentedness and respect that will last you long after the race is over.

Each of you knows right from wrong, and each of you will do right and wrong. All that is important is that you help yourselves and each other to view your mistakes as lessons. You will love yourselves more for having learned and grown. There is no mistake as harmful as the self-hate it can engender if we allow it.

My hope is that you will remember always that you control your life. Whether you are happy, sad, content, frustrated, angry or at peace, it is because you have allowed yourself, or encouraged yourself, to feel the feelings you do.

It is true that any feeling can come upon us initially without our control. We may become saddened by disappointments, but we can overcome our sadness. We may at first be proud of our accomplishments, only to forget them too quickly, yet we can be better to ourselves and take a longer pride in what we have done. We allow ourselves to become frustrated, when a turn of the mind can turn frustrations into joy. What better lesson is there than how long 5 minutes can seem waiting to see a friend, and how short it seems when waiting for something we fear or dread. The difference, of course, is only in our mind. You must learn to control your mind, or it will control you.

I hope you will practice some of what I have written here, and that your practice will make your lives more fulfilling.

Keep your sense of humor. Give others reason to laugh. Spend your time with people who make you laugh. There's no better gift, for them or for you.

Be honest. There is no greater testament to a man's character than his reputation for honesty. More important than testament is that you will find strength in the truth. Lies can follow you forever, and will. The truth does not follow; it leads you, always, to a more fulfilling and peaceful life.

Visualize. Always see yourself succeeding. As the saying goes, if you think you can or if you think you can't, you're probably right. Never lose an opportunity because you didn't give yourself a chance. Do it as if you mean it. You should have a picture in your mind.

Train yourself when you're young to focus on the joys of your life. The mind is a follower and will follow where you lead it. Smile when you're sad and you will begin to feel better. If that fails, do something for someone else. Better yet, do something for someone else first and the smiles will follow naturally.

Be true to yourself. God has worked years to put together a package unlike any other he has created. You have a unique combination of gifts. You need to explore your gifts, and understand that you have them for a reason. There will be many opportunities for you to follow others' footsteps. You must remember that they were not you. Their footsteps will either bore or frustrate you; they will go too far or not far enough. Find your talents, and do what comes naturally for you. Your teachers are messengers only. They are neither better nor worse, only different. Limit yourself to what they have taught you and you have wasted the uniqueness you have to offer to the world.

Have Faith. Those who have faith fare better in every aspect of life; they are better able to cope with its adversities, better able to counsel others in need, to experience the wonder of life's smallest and greatest gifts. Most of all, your faith will give you guidance when you need it most, and an inner peace from the comfort that you are on the right path.

Focus. There is no more important time in your life than now. This was true when you were young and it will be true when you're old. "Now" offers you everything: the chance to enjoy everyone and everything around you; the chance to forget the past and make a new one; to do whatever you're doing as well as you can possibly do it; to correct mistakes. It is the only time we can act on all we have learned from the past; the only time we can prepare for our future. It is the most powerful of times, yet it is the one over which we have most control. Pay attention to the present and your future will reward you.

Look to others to learn. In every person you know there is a lesson for you. Virtually everyone is better at something than you might ever be. It is easy to overlook a strength that's covered with faults, but it's all the more important to search out the strength, to understand the lesson of one who has little else to teach. It enhances the interest we have in every new person we meet, and reminds us that we are all God's children. There is something in the search for the good in others that makes our own goodness easier to find.

Read, but experience. The goal is to experience as much of life as you can. Do things; be as active as you can be. What you see others do, force yourself to try it if it interests you. Don't let others satisfy your need for growth by their own. Teach if you care to teach; play when you're in the mood; travel, experience things that will help you grow, change professions if yours is not fulfilling you. And books? They will help teach you throughout life, help you learn what activities or interests you should pursue next. They show you others' mistakes and accomplishments. They are the grist of life in that they must be worked and ground to their essence. Once done, we can take what they have to offer and try their lessons in our own lives. Always keep a good book within reach. Almost certainly it wants to tell you something that will help you.

Forgive. Anger and resentment drain us of energy and serve only to interfere with our personal growth. If you are angry or resentful to another do what you can to make him your friend. Each of us acts in ways we ourselves don't understand. Your "friend" may hate his actions more than you, and may have more reasons for what he does than you can ever know. Help him if you can. Do your best to forgive; it will make each of you feel better. Only if that fails, and the anger persists, should you leave. Above all, stay away from people who hurt you time and time again. There are millions of others who would love to share you.

Think. The greatest gift of our own struggles is the lesson that others who struggle likely feel as we did when we struggled. How helpful it is to have a kind word, a hug, a help, when we are down. It means as much to your friend, to your family, and sometimes even more ...to a stranger.

There is pollen in the flower. Have you ever looked closely at a flower? There is pollen. It's what attracts the honeybees. It's part of what gives a flower its beauty. Look closely. Pay attention. Look also to the skies and the trees, the grass and the gravel, your friends and your family. Look to the wonders of everyday life, and you will see more in the flower, more in everything, than you had ever dreamed. Force your mind to absorb the "littlest" things in life. By their numbers and beauty, by the wonder of their creation, they will expand your life beyond measure.

Be thankful. "This is good." (Say it to yourself over and over, even when it doesn't seem to be good.) It is common to be thankful for the extraordinary. It is better to be thankful for the ordinary. Every day of our lives we have countless treasures to appreciate. From the time we awaken- that few extra minutes in bed-the sunshine, or the rain, through our window-the warmth or the coolness-the first happy thought we land on-our family, our friends- exercise and rest-sports and news. Every minute, if we appreciate it, adds to the glory of our lives. Don't let them pass unnoticed and unappreciated. Let them treat your mind.

Be considerate. Consider others' feelings, positions, problems and circumstances. Most of us have had difficulties. When you're in a position to do something that affects another human being, be thankful; do what you can to help, not hurt.

Listen. More influence is gained with the ear than the tongue. No one has ever called another ignorant because he listened. No one has ever felt insulted by one who listened. The listener cares; he understands; he appreciates. He learns. His time to speak will come, and they will be ready to listen themselves.

Learn. Pay attention to what you learn. Make a point of thinking of what you want to learn. Remember that respect often comes from what we have learned. Great learning is not only hard work; it is smart work. It involves choices and commitment. It requires sacrifice and the acceptance that our boredom may come from an inability on our part to understand. Work through the boredom; push yourself to expand your world. You can handle everything with time.

Stand up for the weak. Never allow anyone to mistreat another person. There always will be people who seek to take advantage of those with less. Don't let it happen. It should make no difference that some day you may be the person with less.

 Treat yourself well. Do unto yourself as you would have others do unto you. Understand that you will make mistakes, just don't waste them. They can help you learn, they can mold your character, and they can prove to yourself and others around you that each of us can improve and grow. Remember, none of us who loves you thinks you're perfect. Mistakes only exist in the past. Work on who you are, not on what you may or may not have done, and you will love who you become.

Share yourself. The next time you have a chance to help someone, pay attention to how you feel after you've helped. However you describe it, it is a strength that attaches to your character and will serve you when you need it most. It is the feeling of being aligned with goodness, and will help you instill in your own mind that goodness is a part of you.

Trust yourself. Your strength is a unique one. There is none other like it in the universe. You can look to others who have different strengths and wish theirs were yours. You can look past your own strengths to find your weaknesses and wish yours were theirs. But your power and success can only come from the development of your gifts. There will come a time when you must leave the teacher, or you will never move past the teacher. You must decide when.

Always do more. You will always define your work. What must be done, and how? Success is never in completion of a task; it is in the way you complete it. Rarely, if ever, will you feel success unless you have invested more than you ever thought necessary. Steps to success are nothing like those of a ladder, uniform and equidistant; they sometimes come in bunches where the climb is easy. More often, they are placed far apart, making the climb seem not worthwhile. The ladder learns though, and the more rungs you grasp the closer the others will follow.

Choose your priorities carefully. Understand that people who spend their lives chasing a dollar, spend their lives. "Bigger" and "more" are never as much as "enough"". Teach yourself that "enough" is what you have and you will never need, or want, more.

You get what you play for in life. You are gifted. The chances are that you will succeed at what you work at, so work at what you want and what is most worthwhile. Only the outreached hand gets filled; only the entrant wins the race. Think before you reach because your hand will be filled. Choose your races and run against no one. Run only with yourself, as well as you can. Select your goals based on ""want"" not "reach". A person's reach changes and today's reach should have nothing to do with tomorrow's. Reach and play hard.

No goal is more important than its path. Life is a pathway. The value of anything depends on its path. Work more on your paths than on your goals. The importance of a goal is only that it gives direction to your path.

Remember the child. Your parents, your boss, your friends, everyone you will know, however old, is a child. Each of us carries with us questions, insecurities, pains, uncertainties, and the hope that we will do things right. We have all been reprimanded, all been told we've done wrong, and all kept with us the fears of our childhood. Don't be fooled by the person who pretends to have no child in him. Childhood is as much a part of an eighty year old as an eight year old. Remembering this will help you appreciate and accept why he sometimes acts like one.

Tomorrow may never come; yesterday is forever gone. The same is true for next year and last, for the next minute and the last. Enjoy where you are when you are there. Think what you can do now. Last year's problems and next year's fears should not take away today.

Practice. Someday you will have spent "forever" missing shots you should easily make, forgetting things you should know, failing at everything you have mastered. These are the times you should take pride in yourself; they are necessary steps to moving to the next level.

I've written these thoughts as they've occurred to me. No significance is found in their order. Some of them may already have come to you naturally; some may seem unimportant, perhaps even wrong. If there is any value in this list it is that it may help you begin to create your own. Each of us needs our own. Each of us must make our own choices and understand that the smallest of steps begins with choice.

How far we travel, the direction we take, the terrain we must cross, are all consequences of our choices. Whether we travel great distances, whether we move in the right direction, whether the terrain seems easy or difficult depends on choice and commitment.

Work is different from commitment. Commitment is more; it requires work and thought. To say one has practiced tells us little if he has practiced the wrong thing. Or he may have practiced only what he already does well. Commitment means thinking of what is necessary to attain your goals—however difficult it may be—and doing what it takes. Do what you hate if it helps you learn what you love. Find the master in your field and listen. He will help you unwrap your gifts.

Finally, remember that you are never alone. This fact alone should give you the courage you need to live a fulfilling life. Anyone who has the courage to want must also have the courage to lose. And anyone who dares to attempt what others cannot do will eventually fail. I want you to know that failure is not bad. It is neither good nor bad. Whether it becomes good or bad turns on how you respond to failure. As always, you are in control.

Some successes mean nothing unless preceded by failures. Who would Rudy be if he had made Notre Dame's football team easily? He would have been no different from millions of others. His discovery has nothing to do with football. His strength has nothing to do with football. He showed the world that if you reach high enough and long enough, somehow you will grasp what it is that you need. He taught the world, and himself, that success resides in the heart.

Your pride should not come simply from the results of your efforts. These are often not within your control. Instead, pride should come from your efforts alone. They are within your control. They are what become a part of you.

Remember this, and remember that your mom and I love you always. Love, Dad